THE BUS RIDE BACK

THE
BUS
RIDE
BACK

L. A. CARASTRO

Palmetto Publishing Group
Charleston, SC

The Bus Ride Back
Copyright © 2018 by L.A. Carastro
All rights reserved

First Edition

Printed in the United States

ISBN-13: 978-1-64111-188-1
ISBN-10: 1-64111-188-7

CONTENTS

PREFACE

I woke up one morning in Miami, Florida to find my career, my passion, and my sanity extracted from beneath me. Rogue cops manipulated the media and destroyed my police career to cover up their deception and their official misconduct, while attorneys and state prosecutors sought to understand if their behavior actually rose to the level of an illegal/criminal act.

At the end of the day, one glaring question remained: Who are the good guys? And who are the bad guys? I continued on with my life, emotionally distraught.

Not long afterwards, I regained my bearings and launched a new career deeply embedded in the nightlife of the Miami bar business. I flourished for the next twelve years until fate and bad luck found me locked up in a federal prison on drug trafficking charges.

The title of this book refers to the twenty-hour Greyhound bus ride I took back to Miami after completing my federal prison sentence. Sitting in my seat and watching the night move past prompted flashbacks of my life and caused me to relive the events that brought me to that moment.

The magic in this journey brings to light startling revelations that act as a catalyst to transform me back to the person I always was. My passion, my drive, my perseverance, and any good traits I ever had that drove me at a young age to protect and serve the citizens of my city—they returned!

I walked off that Greyhound bus in the early morning hours wielding a newfound hope, desire, and perseverance that would ultimately propel me to a life I could have only imagined.

Overcome by a raging storm, defeated and left for broken, hope would emerge to carry me into the blue skies that lay ahead.

INTRODUCTION

I'm an experienced analog integrated circuit chip designer with a PhD in electrical and computer engineering from the Georgia Institute of Technology. My career spans eighteen years in private industry; I have two patents and six patent applications under review at the present time. I've also written more than fifteen conference papers and presented them at conferences all over the country. However, at forty years of age, I was an out-of-work bartender just returning to Miami after three years in federal prison.

THE BUS RIDE BACK TO MIAMI

Resurrecting my failed life consumed my thoughts as my twenty-hour bus ride from federal prison to the halfway house in Miami progressed. *I want so much to be productive. I want so much to be good at something. Will opportunity ever emerge again?*

As I gazed into the darkness and watched the night slip by, I began to reflect on the past fifteen years and the progression of events leading up to this point in my life. As the bus slowly converged on my destination—as my net worth consisting of T-shirts, underwear, and socks, lay beside me in a duffle bag—it became more and more apparent that my moment was at hand.

The bus began its journey south towards Miami, and we picked up speed, moving off past the lights and driving into the darkness.

Everyone in the dimly lit bus tried to get comfortable and sleep. It was going to be a long night; however, I was wide awake. My thoughts drifted back to the Police Academy, and the beginning of my law enforcement career.

CHAPTER 1
TO PROTECT AND SERVE

LAW ENFORCEMENT CAREER

It was 1973 and I had watched altogether too much Superman and Lone Ranger as a child. Therefore, when I reached the age of twenty-one I decided to make the world safe for women, children, and democracy by becoming a policeman. I was halfway past twenty years old when I entered the Police Academy; when I turned twenty-one, I'd be a fully certified police officer.

I had been living with two policemen for a few years before entering the academy. Most of my friends I associated with were police officers and had been for many years. It was almost like I was already a seasoned police officer when I entered the academy. This scenario had a way of putting me at odds with my fellow police academy students.

I was in excellent physical condition when I went through the academy and did well in academics, amassing a 3.5 grade point average; however, I frequently bumped heads with my fellow students. It was like I was a seasoned professional and they were all rookies. This all came to a head at one point and I was almost expelled from the academy. At this juncture, my police officer friends intervened and kept me enrolled in the academy; however, I was placed on minute-to-minute probation. I was basically told by my supervisors that any slip-ups, and I would be cut from class and wouldn't graduate.

This minute-to-minute probation "sentence" lasted for a month or so until we began firearms training. I had never owned a gun before entering the academy, but firing a weapon came naturally to me. Anything I could see, I could hit with a bullet (and I had twenty-twenty vision). At the completion of firearms training, I had shot a perfect score of three hundred out of three hundred, which was a record held at the academy for several years. I was immediately pulled off minute-to-minute probation and graduated fifth in my class. I also received the only trophy given out at graduation for shooting a perfect three hundred out of three hundred score.

Picture One: Graduation; Firearms Trophy

I was now a certified police officer en route to "my city" to start a new career. About two years later, in January of 1975, my skills with a firearm would come in handy.

I've always had a high regard for human life and tried to preserve it at all cost. The incident described below occurred a couple of years after I joined the force.

DISARMED VIOLENT SUSPECT

This particular night was quiet. The only action was at rush hour and the two accidents I investigated didn't prove to be much. It was about ten o'clock when I received a radio call to respond to a residence—reference, a subject sitting on the front porch waving a gun around in a threatening manner. In my city, when you receive a call like this, the last thing you usually see is the actual subject with a gun. Generally, what happens is the subject flees before you arrive—but not tonight.

I remember as my partner and I approached the house, we were talking about the scuba diving and spear-fishing trip we were planning for the weekend. As we talked, I began to hear someone screaming at us in the distance. I looked around and observed the subject with the gun, seated on the front porch of the house screaming, "If we didn't leave, he would kill us." Reacting immediately, my partner and I split up and positioned ourselves behind some form of cover. I located myself at the northwest corner of the house, which positioned me about twenty feet from the subject at a forty-five-degree angle. My partner positioned himself behind a van parked in the driveway about thirty feet due north of the subject.

The residence was a relatively small four-bedroom one-car-garage home. The subject had positioned himself on the front porch, and seemed to be a middle-aged man, of medium height, dressed in blue

3

jeans and collared short-sleeve shirt. Due to the rambling and slurred speech, I assumed the subject was intoxicated. As the subject brazenly waved the 9-mm weapon at my partner and I, the possibility of death became apparent.

Being a police officer and always carrying a weapon doesn't necessarily emit a feeling of death. But when two guns are involved in a situation, one gun on side *A* side and one gun on side *B*, the feeling of death becomes real.

As I focused in on each moment, I began to hear sounds coming from inside the house. The sounds were voices of young children combined with an older, stronger, female voice that seemed to have a calming effect on the children. I began to think that this could be a despondent father's attempt to reach out for help, yet in his drunken stupor he was creating a situation that could lead to his immediate execution—that would be horribly witnessed and relived by his loved ones. As I drew my weapon, I realized that I must somehow disarm this man before events went too far.

As I stood with my gun trained on the subject, I began to put together what needed to be done. This was my call and my responsibility, and I had to disarm the subject without harm to him or my partner. I attempted to gain help from my supervisor by trying to radio him, but for some reason he was unavailable. Seconds moved likes minutes as the situation unfolded.

As I stood at the corner of the house, the subject began pivoting back and forth, pointing the gun at me and then at my partner. I noticed several neighbors gathering across the street as if what they were seeing was confined to the opposite side. Just as I became concerned for their wellbeing, several police units arrived and they dispersed. I tried to raise my supervisor on the radio again with negative results, while the muffled cries from inside the house echoed in the night.

As time progressed, the use of deadly force became increasingly imminent. The subject had already pointed the gun at me, which constitutes the use of deadly force. I was also not sure how many more times I could look down the barrel of his gun without reacting. Keeping in mind the consequences in regard to his family, I couldn't help but think about my own family, and the impact it would have on them should something happen to me. Having had my gun elevated in the ready-to-fire position for twenty minutes now, fatigue was beginning to set in. The weight of the gun seemed to be increasing exponentially.

My partner, by this time, was getting anxious. He had peeked his head around the side of the van several times, and each time, was threatened by the subject not to do it again. All of a sudden, as if overcome by frustration, my partner bolted from behind the van and raced toward the subject in an attempt to physically subdue him. Needing to cover thirty feet, he didn't have much of a chance to succeed. The subject reacted immediately by raising his gun, cocking the hammer, and beginning to squeeze the trigger. Now my partner was almost at point-blank range, with no chance of a missed shot by the subject. I had my gun trained on the subject for twenty minutes now, and the weapon felt like a cannon. I knew it was too late to fire at the subject, a mere reflex action would send a 9-mm bullet piercing through my partner.

It seemed like I had waited too long and had let the situation develop too far. Now the life of my partner was on the line, and at point-blank range, there was little chance of a miss. The only hope left was to shoot the gun out of his hand and, being one of the best shots in the country, I had the ability and the confidence to do it. I was never more focused on each passing second in my life. I took a deep breath, aimed in on the hammer mechanism just above his hand, and fired. My gun seemed to explode in my hand; billows of smoke and flames shot out from all sides. The gun's recoil threw it high in the air. My arms felt like rubber; I held on with all I had. The subject's gun was blown clear from his hand. He retrieved the weapon and attempted to fire, but was unable. When my bullet struck the hammer mechanism of his gun, it had blown the firing pin to pieces and made the gun inoperable. I was having difficulty seeing through the smoke from my weapon. As I approached the subject, I observed my fellow officers subduing him. The problem was over, the subject was unharmed, and my partner was very much alive.

I turned and proceeded up the porch stairs into the house, where I was met by a middle-aged woman surrounded by three young children, who were all clinging to her. I advised her that the subject was subdued and unharmed. She explained to me that he was her brother who had been in and out of jail all his life. He had come over that evening to borrow money from her and when she refused, went on a rampage. She stated that I should have killed him; it would have saved a lot of people a lot of trouble. It seemed that I had read this situation a little wrong, but at least the kids hadn't seen Uncle Who-Knows-What lose his brains on their front porch.

After obtaining all the pertinent information, I returned to the police station. I was met by my partner, who was in the process of calming his nerves. It seemed that as he was lunging for the subject, he observed what he thought was a mussel flash coming from the barrel of the subject's gun. It was actually the sparks created by my bullet ricocheting off the subject's gun. My partner believed that he had been shot and had spent the next several minutes searching his body for a bullet hole.

I received the Officer of the Month Award, which included ten hours paid leave and the opportunity to attend the monthly Kiwanis

Club luncheon. The subject, apparently, was nothing like what I had first surmised. He had an extensive criminal past, having been convicted and jailed on burglary, robbery, and murder charges. He was again convicted of attempted murder and sentenced to ten years.

POLICE DEPARTMENT

MEMORANDUM:

To: Officer L. Carastro

From: Police Chief　　　　　　　　　　　　Date: 4 MAR 76

Subject: Officer of the Month for February 1976

The Awards Committee has selected you as Officer of the Month for February 1976.

This selection was based on our performance in Case No. xx xxxx in which you responded to a call reference to a subject who was threatening others with a gun. When subject pointed his gun at a fellow officer, you were successful in shooting the gun from his hand, subduing him and placing him under arrest.

You are commended for your good police work and are hereby awarded an additional ten (10) hours of Annual leave. A copy of this memo will be placed in your personnel file.

Picture Two: Officer of the Month Award

I was satisfied with the way I'd handled myself that night. It gave me a great deal of insight into my personality. It showed me a potentially strong point, as well as a potentially weak point. By this, I mean that in stressful situations I have the ability to concentrate and think on my feet. As far as first impressions go, I need a lot of work.

The following day after shooting the gun from the guy's hand, the chief called me into his office. I was expecting a pat on the back for not killing one of our citizens and generating bad press for the city; instead, I was chastised for not killing the man. The police chief stated, "Who do you think you are? The Lone Ranger?" He also said, "When we pull our gun, we use it—deadly force." He finished by saying, "What if all the criminals think we're going to shoot the guns out of their hands when they commit crimes?" For obvious reasons, I agreed with the chief and quickly left his office (with a strange feeling in my heart). I acknowledged that I would never do it again.

Our chief of police had been chief for many years. He had grown up in law enforcement; that might help to explain his views on the use of "deadly force."

MY CITY'S BANK ROBBERY

A couple of months later that same year, we had a bank robbery in my city. There were two victims impacted by this bank robbery: Tippy, the informant, who was killed by my city's police, and me—I was ultimately disgraced by the media and fired due to my knowledge of unethical and possible criminal behavior on part of my city's police detectives. I'll be referencing the actual newspaper articles from the *Miami Herald* that were published about these events (see articles one through eleven). I'll also be listing the exact location of the text in these articles that coincides with the statements I'm making about these occurrences.[1]

Disclaimer: I want to make it clear, that my city did not condone this type of behavior from its police officers. The unethical and possible

---

[1]   All of these articles have been purchased from the original publisher; they can now be re-published here (license agreement #REF 000054059). All articles have names, places, and individuals names removed for legal reasons, and are available for the reader to peruse in the appendix.

criminal behavior documented in these news-paper articles (including my eyewitness accounts) was executed by "rogue cops."

The neighboring city policeman involved in setting up this event was relieved of duty and forced to resign from his city's Police Department shortly after the occurrence (see article seven). The police officer from my city also involved in setting up this robbery was again involved in setting up a robbery that resulted in one of his informants being shot and killed two years later (see article eight).

THIS IS HOW IT WENT DOWN

In the winter of 1975 at ten o'clock in the morning, three men walked into a Federal savings and loan bank brandishing guns and demanded money from the tellers. All three men were shot by my city's and the neighboring city's police officers as they exited the bank. One man was killed, and two were taken into custody to local area hospitals in critical condition (see article one). The bank robber who was killed, was actually the police informant who was working in cooperation with my city's and the neighboring city's detectives (see article two, paragraph A) and had, as instructed, notified police prior to the robbery by phoning in an anonymous tip that the bank was going to be robbed (see article one, paragraph B; article three, paragraph E).

GUARDING THE BANK ROBBERY
SUSPECT IN HOSPITAL OVERNIGHT

It was a Friday, in the winter of 1975. I checked into service at 10 p.m. and was on my way to a local area Hospital to guard an inmate prisoner who had been shot earlier that day while robbing a bank (see article one, paragraph A). My task that evening was to spend the night in ICU and make sure the bank robbery suspect remained in custody while the doctors worked on his life-threating injuries.

Holdup Suspect Dies Behind Police Line Outside   Federal's   Branch

Police Gun Drop Robber

When I arrived in the suspect's ICU room, I found him asleep, so I got a chair and made myself comfortable just outside his room in the hallway. An hour or so had gone by when I noticed he was just waking up. I looked in on him and saw that he was staring up at the ceiling, mumbling something about the failed bank robbery, and sad that his accomplice and friend "Tippy" had been killed. He kept saying that he didn't want to rob the bank; Tippy kept hounding him to do it. On two occasions, all three perpetrators had driven by the bank; he kept saying that the bank "just looked so easy; there were never any guards around."

DETECTIVES SET UP BURGLARIES USING TIPPY

While listening to the suspect speak, I started to think back to the first time I'd seen Tippy. You see, he had been a police informant for quite some time. I had first seen Tippy several months earlier; he had set up a burglary in one of my city's upscale single-family neighborhoods.

I was told by a detective who recruited me to work under-cover with him that Tippy had been working with my city's detectives, setting up home burglaries. They had arrested him on a previous burglary and had made a deal with him, that if he worked with them (setting up more home burglaries) they would not arrest him for the first burglary they had caught him on.

So, Tippy would go out into his neighborhood and talk several guys into committing a home burglary in my city. The detectives would use a house on the vacation list (i.e., homeowners would call the Police Department and ask that they keep an eye on their house while they were on vacation).

Then Tippy would drive to the house, drop the guys off at a predetermined point told to him by the police detectives. Tippy would also tell the guys where to enter the house (as told to him by the detectives), then drive away in his car. He would then return several minutes later to pick them up. When Tippy returned to pick the guys up with the stolen property from the house, the police detectives, who had been staking out the house, would jump out of their cars and arrest all the guys.

Tippy was also instructed to call the police department's complaint desk fifteen minutes before he arrived at the house to make the whole operation look like some *anonymous informant* had apprised them of the crime. I know all this because one of the detectives recruited me to work undercover with him one night, on one of these operations. I was told about how Tippy worked with them to set up

11

and bust burglars; however, I wasn't told about this till after the first burglary I witnessed.

Therefore, after chasing down and arresting all the perpetrators (except for Tippy, who always escaped) and writing up all the paperwork, we then sat around in the office and talked about what we had done. At this point, I was told how the operation worked, and how Tippy always got away to set up another burglary.

Before being told how the burglary "setup" worked, my original thoughts were that the detectives were extremely good at what they did and were experienced enough to foil this type of crime—boy, was I wrong!!

BACK AT THE HOSPITAL, GUARDING THE BANK ROBBERY SUSPECT

Listening to the suspect reminisce about his past criminal life (before the bank robbery), and how much jail time had cost him, he said that he really hadn't wanted to commit this crime. Our suspect had been released from a Florida State Prison a couple of years earlier for his most recent conviction. While in jail, he took some vocational classes and learned how to write as a journalist. He had actually been working in south Florida for a local newspaper writing a weekly column, and he seemed to be turning his life around.

The suspect continued to regret committing this crime. Tippy was dead and he was all shot up. He kept saying that Tippy had basically talked him into it. It had taken about six months for Tippy to do this, and after driving by and going into the bank on two occasions and not seeing any guards—how easy a robbery it might be—and he was talked into it. While looking at the wounded suspect and listening to him speak, all I was thinking about was, *Did my city's detectives have a role in setting up this crime? Just like what they did with Tippy and the home burglaries?*

At about five in the morning or so, the Miami Herald morning edition was out, and I had picked up a copy. On the front page, it had the bank robbery and a picture of Tippy—shot to death by my city's and the neighboring city's Police Departments (see article two). On the front page, the headline was "Police Kill Informant In Foiled Bank Robbery." The suspect didn't know at that point that Tippy was the informant, so I decided to show him the newspaper. His exact words were "that under-the-rock living motherfucker"! He was not happy; however, I thought he should know who his so-called good friend was before he died.

DETECTIVES SET UP THE BANK ROBBERY

The next day I checked into my shift at the police station, I spoke with the detective who had recruited me to work undercover with him the night I first saw Tippy, and he told me what had actually gone down.

First, the police detectives were getting bored with setting up and arresting burglary suspects; they wanted a more serious crime. A robbery was more serious than a burglary and would look better on their work performance record (see article four, paragraph B). So, they got in touch with Tippy again and told him to go out and find several guys and stage a robbery (just like he did for the burglaries).

The next question was what to rob? The police detectives thought that a bank robbery would yield the "career impact" they were looking for, so they found an out-of-the-way bank in our city (surrounded by trees; it didn't even look like a bank), and they would stage their bank robbery there. Then, Tippy went out in search of accomplices. He found several in his neighborhood; however, he needed someone with experience. So, he ventured down to Homestead, Florida and tried to bring in our suspect, who I ended up guarding in the hospital.

The detective also told me that on at least two occasions, Tippy piled all the guys into his car and drove to the bank they were going to rob. The police detectives were advised and contacted the guards at the bank and told them not to be in plain sight when the bank robbers came by (or something to that effect). Therefore, when Tippy and the guys drove by the bank, it looked like it wasn't guarded very well and perhaps would be easy to rob. Tippy and the guys did this several times over the six-month period while my suspect was deciding to rob or not to rob (just like he explained to me in the hospital). At one point, Tippy's car broke down, so the gang needed to replace it with another car. This is when the police detectives came forward again and gave Tippy an unmarked detective bureau car to use in the bank robbery (see article five, paragraph B; article six, paragraph G; article ten, paragraph F).

Finally, my suspect decided to join the gang and rob the bank. It had taken Tippy six months to talk him into it. This was when Tippy realized that the gang had no guns to use in the bank robbery, so the police detectives came forward again and gave Tippy several guns from the police property room to use in the bank robbery (per the detective who had recruited me to work undercover with him). As it turns out, the police detectives would ultimately supply the bank robbers with 1) the bank; 2) the vehicle; and 3) the guns to rob the bank.

THE BANK ROBBERY

The day of the bank robbery, at about ten in the morning, Tippy and his accomplices arrived at the bank driving the police detective car and wielding the guns from the police property room. Just like when Tippy had done the burglaries, he phoned in an anonymous phone call to the police station and advised that a bank robbery was going to occur at a particular time and place (see article one, paragraph B; article three, paragraph E). I remember being told by other police officers that the police station basically emptied out, i.e., all officers responded to the bank robbery location armed and ready to shoot the perpetrators. The scene probably looked like the last scene of *Butch Cassidy and the Sundance Kid*. Butch and Sundance were executed by the Bolivian army.

The police department claim (see article three, paragraph B) that Tippy got shot because he was wearing a ski mask, and therefore, they couldn't see his face. However, the defense attorney for surviving suspects had proof that Tippy was *not* wearing a mask (see article five, paragraph D).

I believe this is how Tippy got shot. Twenty or so police officers from my city and the neighboring city —all of whom had never seen Tippy before—armed with shot guns surrounded the bank (under cars and on top of roofs and in trees; see articles one and two) waiting for the bank robbers to exit the bank. If only the detectives who were involved in the planning of the bank robbery had been there—they all knew Tippy—he would not have been shot. It would have gone down like the setup burglaries: All would have been arrested except for Tippy, and he would have driven away.

FIRED FROM THE POLICE DEPARTMENT

I was (ultimately) fired from my city's police department in November of 1976 for conduct unbecoming a police officer by allowing my roommate to date a fifteen-year-old girl; he was thirty years old. To make a long story short, he was a swimming instructor/life guard at a popular

Miami hotel and she was a fifteen-going-on-twenty-five-year-old girl. Her father had no problem with my roommate dating his daughter, however my police chief did.

I believe the actual reason I was fired from the department was because of the Tippy bank robbery shooting, which occurred in the winter of 1975.

While doing research for this book, I now have a clear understanding of what is legal and what is not legal concerning the police/informant relationship (see article six, paragraph D). The assistant State Attorney (who was investigating the bank robbery), refers to the type of police work that my city and the neighboring city were engaged in as "deception," and was deemed by the neighboring city Police Chief as "official misconduct" on part of the police officers. As a result, the police Chief relieved one of the officers who supervised the bank robbery of his duties (forced to resign) in December of 1975 (see article six, paragraph B).

In article eight, the author describes how my city's police department would "plot with their informant a crime that might otherwise not have occurred." They write, "[E]vidence indicates that the police department encouraged [their informants] to lure other men into [committing a criminal act]. . . . It is one thing for police, told by an informant that a crime is to be committed, to stake out the scene and attempt to prevent it. But it comes perilously close to entrapment for police to instigate the crime through their informant."

I now understand the magnitude of what was going on and what led to my firing.

The progression of events is listed below.

#	DATES	DETAILS
1	Aug. 1974	I want no part of the Tippy burglary setup.
2	Mar. 1975	Seven months later Tippy is killed during the bank robbery.
3	1975-76	Attorneys for bank robbery suspects, and State Attorney are digging into how police handled the bank robbery/Tippy killing.
		Neighboring city detective is forced to resign.
		Begins to look like someone, or some group in authority, might be charged with a serious crime.
		I'm a liability for police officers responsible for setting up bank robbery and manipulating Tippy.
		They believe I can help prosecutors' understanding of what transpired. They don't realize that's the farthest thing from my mind.
4	Feb. 1976	My city's police department gets information about my roommate and his underage girlfriend.
5	Mar. 1976	My chief fires me for conduct unbecoming of a police officer because of my roommate and his girlfriend.
6	Sept. 1976	My chief violates civil service laws in an effort to fire me quickly. I sue and get reinstated with several months backpay, but damage has been done.
		After being reinstated, I'm suspended immediately, with pay pending a trial board hearing.
7	Nov. 1976	Two weeks later I lose the city trial board hearing; my firing is upheld.

Basically, I knew too much about this "deception/official misconduct" police practice (see article six, paragraph D) and didn't want to be part of their group; however, at the time I didn't realize how they were acting qualified as deception or official misconduct. If the federal or state government ever set out to prosecute any of the detectives for what happened to Tippy, I would have been a good federal or state witness. I never considered that scenario; however, I believe some of the folks at my department did . . . and they acted on it.

The two attorneys for the suspects and the state attorney were breathing down police departments' necks trying to get to the bottom of what actually occurred at the bank. I believe the state attorney was trying to understand if "deception/official misconduct" actually met the criteria for what would be considered an illegal/criminal act on the part of the police. This must have been very uncomfortable for the primaries involved.

So, in March of 1976, my department decided to not only fire me but discredit me to the public, using the news media. I was written about in the newspaper and I was filmed on the evening news. My department claimed that I'd had sex with my roommate's fifteen-year-old girl friend, even though there was no evidence—even the fifteen-year-old girl stated that we had never had sex. She was my roommate's girlfriend; I never would and never did have sex with her.

The Assistant State Attorney was also called in to investigate the case and found nothing to prosecute. Therefore, there were never any criminal charges lodged against me—just unsubstantiated allegations to the media and an internal firing.

In their rush to discredit me, the police chief purposely ignored the legal process in firing a civil servant, knowing I would take the illegal firing to court and be reinstated with back pay. I believe they needed to act on my "credibility as a state witness" as soon as possible to circumvent any possibility of me becoming a viable witness for the prosecution if the state decided to indict the police officers involved.

In March of 1976, I was illegally fired, and in September of 1976, re-hired with all back pay; however, I was immediately put on suspension awaiting a trial board hearing.

In November of 1976, a four-hour internal five-member trial board was convened; the vote was four to one to uphold the firing. One member of the trial board (a lawyer) agreed with me that I should not be fired, and that there was no evidence of any wrongdoing on my part. The lawyer also stated that when the trial board's decision was appealed in state court, it would be overturned. However, I never made it to state court; I ran out of money to defend myself.

It seems that the detective who had tried to recruit me into the detective bureau early on had also suggested an attorney for me to use to fight the firing. Filing needless submissions to the court and going to federal court instead of state court to plead my case basically ran me out of money. My lawyer originally took my case to federal court and it cost a lot of money for him to do this. I found out later that he should have taken my case to state court. We would have gotten relief in state court, not federal court. That's also what the federal court judge stated: "Why are you bringing this to me and not to a state court? You have a good chance of relief in state court."

So, after a year of fighting to get my job back and clear my name, I basically walked away from my city's police department; it had cost me all the money I had. The chief also wanted to take my police certification, which meant I would not be certified to work as a police officer anywhere else in the state. When advised of this, I basically handed over to them the certification; I never wanted to be a law enforcement officer again. So, at twenty-five years of age, I had no more law enforcement career, and no money.

My city's police department had accomplished what they had set out to do: They discredited me to the public using the news media and they took away my law enforcement career (actually, I handed it back to them). I was now no longer a liability because I knew about the "deception/official misconduct" activities going on in the police department. If the federal or state government ever set out to prosecute any of the detectives for killing Tippy (due to their "deception/official misconduct" police tactics), I would not be a good federal or state witness; I would be a disgruntled ex-employee. However, a year after I had been fired in the winter of 1978, the police detectives again killed their informant in a botched restaurant robbery (see article nine).

This time Janet Reno (state attorney) convened a grand jury to investigate the city's police practices (see articles ten and eleven). The grand jury criticized the police handling of the robbery stakeout and denounced the leadership of the city's police department (see article eight, editorial). However, no charges were filed against the officers involved in the actual shooting. It seemed once again, the detectives who organized and set up the robbery lost control of the situation at a critical time, resulting in the death of the informant—just like Tippy in the bank robbery.

Question: In article three, paragraph B, the police claim that Tippy was shot by mistake because he was wearing a ski mask and the officers didn't know who he was. Then why was the second informant killed asked by the police detectives to make a mask and wear it during the robbery (per Article ten, paragraph D)? This particular detective was one of the organizers of the bank robbery in which Tippy was killed because he wore a ski mask.

One question remains: Who are the good-guys and who are the bad-guys? And is the line that separates the two "blurred" in some cases when "rogue cops" are involved.

Articles one through eleven are written about both robberies where their informants were killed. The names of the cities, policemen, hospitals, and locations have been removed for legal reasons.[2]

---

2   These articles were purchased from the Miami Herald; the dates of the articles range from March 1975 to May 1978.

CHAPTER 2
A TIME TO MOVE ON

BACK IN THE BUS

A few hours had gone by when the bus slowed down and pulled into an all-night diner. Everyone, still half asleep, stumbled off the bus and up to the counter for a quick meal. The coffee was good, the eggs were greasy, the highway cop was off in the corner talking to the waitress. Thirty minutes later, it was time to board the bus and continue our journey.

The engine strained as the bus accelerated to its max speed. This speed made you feel like you would reach your destination sooner rather than later, somewhat euphoric at finally making good time and the destination was closer; however, my case was different—I didn't know what I was going to do with my life after I stepped off that bus.

So, I leaned back in my seat and let my thoughts drift off again, this time to my bar career; how it began, the people I encountered, and a chance meeting that would put me face to face with who would turn out to be my best friend and love of my life.

Her name is Sheri Decca and the world seemed to stop as soon as our eyes met. This was a glimpse into my future, coming just after being destroyed by "my city's" Police Department. I would fall madly in love with Sheri, and ultimately spend the rest of my life with her; how-ever, none of that would happen for another sixteen years.

POLICE CAREER ENDS; BAR CAREER BEGINS

It was time for me to move on and reinvent myself at age twenty-five—as what, I had no idea. I was a degreed law enforcement professional with an excellent work record (except for the firing), who was not cer-tified to work in the industry. I had no other skills, and the bad press I got at the hands of the police department and the news media left very few, if any, prospects.

As a police officer, my job was to protect and serve the citizens of my city at any expense. I took an oath to stand between any situation that could potentially harm anyone I was sworn to protect.

This was my job description and my life's passion; I was sworn to protect and serve and that's exactly what I did, no matter what the per-sonal cost. I kept myself in the best physical shape, and always scored perfect at the firing range. I always wanted to be sure that I was mental-ly and physically prepared for any unexpected incident.

But after the events of the past several months, after losing not only my career but my life's passion, I felt lost. Some of my firemen friends wanted me to join the Miami-Dade Fire Department, but then, I was in no hurry to step back into a civil-service job. I felt empty, like I had no purpose anymore, like I didn't care anymore.

However, after about a month or so of looking for a job, I got a phone call from an old friend. His name was Vince Marciano and he owned a pizza parlor in South Miami. For years, several neighborhood kids and I used to hang out at his pizza parlor. We were all very good friends. Vince called me one day and said that he knew me, and that I was a great guy. He also said, "No one, not even the city's police department or news media could make me think any different!" Vince said that he was leaving the pizza business and buying a bar in Miami Springs (Hunter's Lounge), and he wanted to know if I would like to work for him as a bartender. I thought this job would be perfect; responsible only for the few people sitting at my bar. I could basically disappear into the Miami nightlife without a care in the world.

Vince had thrown me a lifeline. I jumped at the chance to work behind the bar and began work immediately. Vince was in the process of buying the bar, which was a very popular neighborhood dance club. The year was 1977 and my bar career had begun. I would stay in this field for the next twelve years and prosper.

SHERI APPEARS . . . AND TIME STANDS STILL

After about six months into my bartending career, I was working a weekend night and it was about eleven o'clock. I heard a girl screaming at me over the bar, "Look at that bartender!" It was a very busy night, five deep at the bar, however I could hear her screams over the loud music. I looked up and saw this beautiful girl standing in front of the dance floor, about ten feet away from the bar, a can light in the ceiling shining down on her. She was surrounded by people, but she looked like she was standing there alone. This was my first glimpse of Sheri! She had a drink in her hand and was looking directly at me and smiling. All of a sudden it seemed like the room fell silent; nothing was moving except for Sheri. She was smiling at me, her big eyes simmering under the can light. They talk about time standing still, but I had never really experienced it like this. Maybe when I shot the gun out of the guy's hand when I was a policeman, but not like this.

Suddenly, as quickly as she had emerged from the crowd, Sheri was gone. However, she would return in my life as my soulmate, best friend, and wife, forever. I think life can be a little funny like that. Sheri was standing right in front of me in 1977; we married in 1994, and have been married for the past twenty-four years.

Picture Three: Sheri Decca Carastro in Beauty School, 1984

I finished out the year working for Vinnie at Hunter's Lounge, tending bar. I learned a lot that year and really enjoyed my new career. I was involved with another girl at the time, so I couldn't pursue Sheri. I did find out that we had both grown up in Westchester (in South Miami), a couple of blocks from one another, and that my younger sister knew Sheri very well.

In December of that year, I would move to Tampa to open my own bar. I never forgot seeing Sheri. She remained in my dreams for the next several years.

GRAHAM'S LOUNGE, TAMPA, FLORIDA

Near the end of 1977, I got a visit from Eddie and Mike Graham and my cousin Doug, all of who were from Tampa. Eddie Graham was a professional wrestler and the Owner and President of the NWA (National Wrestling Alliance) and Championship Wrestling from Florida. Mike Graham (Eddie's son) was also a big wrestling star and worked for his Dad; Mike, Doug, and I were all the same age. I grew up in Miami and Mike and Doug grew up in Tampa. My dad's family was all from Tampa, so I'd go there every summer and spend time with Doug and Mike; we all were very close.

Eddie, Mike, and Doug had flown down to Miami in Eddie's plane for a bench-press contest. I picked them up at the airport and we all went to the contest. Mike and Doug were competing, and I was just watching. If I remember right, Mike won his division and Doug came in third in his division. After the contest, we went to Hunter's Lounge (where I worked) to have a few drinks before they flew back to Tampa. When Mike found out that I was in the bar business, he said, "I'll buy one [a bar] and you can manage it for me." I told him I knew all about the business (which was a big lie) and I'd definitely relocate to Tampa and manage the bar for him when he bought it. I was thinking I would never hear about this again; however, I was wrong! Two weeks later, Mike got ahold of me and said that he had bought the bar and he wanted me to come up to Tampa immediately and run it. So, off I went to Tampa to manage the bar. Tampa was a tough town, so I brought my bouncer (Steve Smith) from Hunter's with me so I wouldn't get beaten up or killed by some crazy Port Tampa patron.

The bar Mike had bought had been an Italian restaurant that had a small ten-stool horseshoe bar in the lounge portion of the restaurant. To transform the old Italian restaurant into a disco-type dance club would require a major redesign. This is where my words came back to haunt me. I had said I knew all about the bar business, so Mike figured that I should know how to design the new disco lounge . . . I didn't. What I ultimately did was lock myself in the building, took several hits of speed to stay awake for three days, bought a sketch pad and several colored pencils, and proceeded to map out an efficient, money-making establishment.

I had learned from the best at Hunter's Lounge. Vince had bought the bar from Dick Wise; Dick was an ex-City of Miami policeman. He found out, in the early 1960s that if an existing bar had an outstanding tax lien on it, you could pay off the lean and own the liquor license. So Dick got with Joe Flannigan (of Big Daddy's Lounges), who had a lot of money, and started buying up bars in Miami. Dick and Joe became innovators in the bar business. They opened 135 bar/lounges all over Florida, Georgia, California, Philadelphia, and Tennessee. Dick and Joe were basically the fathers of what we know today as "the bar business."

When Vince bought Hunter's from Dick Wise, Dick stayed with the bar for a few months to show Vince how things needed to run to make money. When I worked with Dick, I learned the bar business from basically the best, so when I locked myself in Graham's Lounge and did the redesign, I really had a good idea of what we needed to do and how to do it. I had learned a lot from Dick Wise!

I designed a big dance floor and elevated area, and two big oval bars with sixty bar stools around them. I also had a ladies night on Thursday night, where ladies drank for free and the guys paid a cover charge to get in. It worked beautifully. Everyone had fun Thursday night and it carried over into the weekend, and even through the week.

We opened the new Graham's Lounge in the spring of 1977, and in less than a month, we had lines around the place with people trying to get in; it was a great success. I had lost everything I owned, including my law enforcement career, a few months earlier; however, I had successfully begun a new career and was headed for bigger and better things. But I was now living in Tampa, and on my infrequent trips back and forth to Miami, I hadn't seen Sheri again. Safe to say, though, I hadn't forgotten about her!

RETURN TO MIAMI

I stayed in Tampa for the next several years. Graham's Lounge was a success and I was making a good name for myself in the bar business there. In 1980, Mike's wife caught him cheating on her and threatened a costly divorce. Mike and I were partners in the bar, so we decided to sell. Mike kept his marriage intact and I went back to Miami.

A couple of friends of mine I grew up with, Billy and Joe, had just bought a bar named Zachery's. It had a little bit older crowd but was basically the same format as Graham's. We had a disc jockey that played top-forty tunes. I tended bar with a guy named T. B. in the day time and on Sunday night. It was a great crowd; it was really fun working there.

My first night when I started, I asked Joe if there were any rules. He responded by saying, "Yes, there's just one rule: We don't take shit—we give shit." And that's how it went. It was a bartender's bar; the world revolved around us, and we ran everything, made lots of money and had lots of fun! I stayed at Zachary's for a couple of years, then decided to move on and work with Michael Taylor at a bar called Rainbows.

Michael was a very good friend of mine; I had met him right when I'd gotten into the bar business back in the Hunter's days. Michael was the best bartender I had ever seen. They had a "Best Bartender in the Country Contest" back in 1977 and Michael came in second—that's how good he was. Below is a picture of Michael in 1977 on the cover of Miami Magazine after the contest.

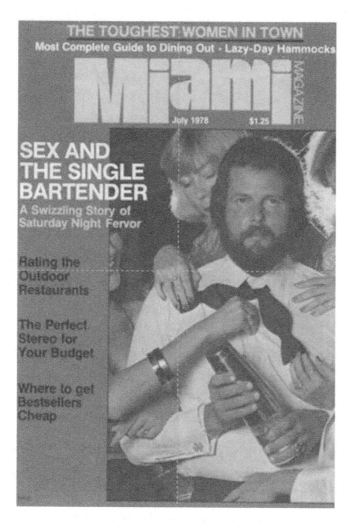

Picture Four: Michael Taylor on the Cover of Miami Magazine

Michael knew everyone, and everyone loved Michael. It wasn't just about getting drinks over the bar (which he also did very well). It just felt so good being around him, and he attracted other people you would feel really good being around. Whenever you were in the bar when Michael was working, you felt at home. It was great drinking with him.

Michael was now working at Rainbows Restaurant and Bar, and it was sort of a dream of mine to work with him someday. That day was here, and I was working with Michael. What I didn't realize was that Sheri was the owner of Rainbows—and I found this out at the first employee meeting.

FACE TO FACE WITH SHERI

It seemed that while I was in Tampa for those few years, Sheri had met, dated, and married George Jay. His father had died and left him a thriving movie studio business. George's business was connected to a movie studio in North Miami Beach, and handled all the transportation and living facilities for the actors while they were on-site making a movie.

Sheri had always wanted a bar, and unbeknownst to me, was also really good friends with Michael Taylor. When we saw each other again for the first time at the first employee meeting, I think both of our hearts stopped. However, Sheri was married, and I had also recently gotten married.

Rainbows was located in South Miami, and gorgeous; however, it had no business—it was new. We had a great band and the food was five-star, but it took us about three months to get the place going. Rainbows, in its heyday, boasted a very unique clientele. Everybody who was anybody came to our bar. We had lawyers, judges, drug dealers, bookies, college and professional sports figures, and because George was in the movie business, we had movie stars and models.

The producers of the movie *Scarface* were actually going to use Rainbows in the movie for the bar scene and the shoot-out. However, the Cuban population who'd come to the US in the 1960s didn't want to be associated with the Cubans who came over during the 1980 Mariel boatlift—which was what the movie was about.

During the Mariel boatlift in 1980, Castro announced that all Cubans wishing to emigrate to the US would be free to board boats at the port of Mariel (west of Havana). So every Cuban with a boat— or could *find* a boat—set out for the Port of Mariel to pick up their grandparents, siblings, aunts, uncles, and cousins. The only catch was that Castro made them take two additional people per family member with them to the US—people who had either been released from Cuban jails or were mentally insane. Before the United States realized what had happened, these former prisoners and mentally insane people were released on the streets of Miami. Many of the Mariel refugees were very good, upstanding people, but the former prisoners/mentally insane set off a huge crime wave in Miami, up until they were eventually recaptured and jailed.

Due to the negative publicity centered around the drugs and violence in Miami (largely coming from the unwanted Mariel refugees), the city decided not to shoot the movie in Miami. However, some of the scenes had to be shot there, such as the shooting scene on Ocean Drive on South Beach.

Back at Rainbows, we had a 6 a.m. liquor license, which meant that we were open later than most any of the other bars in Miami. As all the other bars closed in Miami, everyone converged on Rainbows because they could drink till six in the morning. This meant we also would get all the bar people when the earlier bars closed; we were basically the last stop. I worked for the next two years with Michael and Sheri at

Rainbows, and we made tons of money, more than I had ever made in the bar business.

Picture Five: Fishing Boat Loaded with Cuban Refugees Heads Towards Key West

Michael and I were household names in the South Miami bar scene, and whenever we went out on our days off, everything was free; we never paid for a drink, but we always way over-tipped. The folks who worked in the bar always loved to see Michael and I come in; they always knew they were going to have lots of fun and make lots of money that night.

During the time at Rainbows, Sheri and I also became very good friends. I grew to really admire Sheri. I saw her in a variety of situations and she was always a "lady"—elegant! Sheri was beautiful on the inside and outside.

I would ultimately disappear again, this time into the mountains of Vermont for a year to save my friend's life. During that time, my first marriage failed. Since Sheri was "taken" (married), my new quest in life was to find a girl just like Sheri, now that I knew what to look for. Sheri was basically the girl of my dreams and I was in search of another one just like her. I would come to realize that there was only one Sheri—no other.

RICK ESCAPES MIAMI

One night after working at Rainbows, at about four in the morning, I stopped by one of our favorite bars to have a cocktail before going home and ran into Eddie "The Cockroach." Eddie and his family immigrated from Cuba in the early 1960's and had grown up in Miami. He was a waiter at the David Williams Hotel in Miami and a very good friend of mine. We had nick-named him "The Cockroach" years earlier, not sure why. However, tonight he had terrible news about one of our good friends, Rick Foster.

He said that the FBI had called Rick and told him they had a warrant for his arrest for drug trafficking (see article twelve). It seemed that Rick had been driving kilos of cocaine to Aspen, Colorado, for the past several years. The FBI agent told Rick they were around the corner from his house and they would be by to arrest him in several minutes. They asked Rick to be outside alone and be ready to go to jail. Below is the newspaper clipping about Rick's arrest.

This was a common practice for the FBI; they would call the suspect when they got close to the house and ask if the suspect would step outside and be ready to go to jail when they got there. This would get the suspect away from the wife, kids, and dog, and make it easier for the FBI to do their job. However, sometimes the suspect is not ready to be jailed, and flees the scene and basically goes on the run as a fugitive. That was the case with Rick—he was not ready to go to jail that day.

Drug suspect held on $5.5 million bond

MIAMI — A man sought on 1984 federal drug indictments in Denver and St. Louis was ordered held on $5.5 million bond Thursday by a federal magistrate pending a removal hearing.

The U.S. Marshals Service said   was arrested Wednesday night at his home in the Kendale Lakes area outside of Miami.

According to warrants presented before U.S. Magistrate Samuel Smargon,   was one of six people sought by Denver authorities for conspiracy to distribute cocaine. One overt act mentioned in the indictment was delivering cocaine to Aspen, Colo.

He also was named in a warrant charging be was one of five people indicted in St. Louis on another drug conspiracy charge.

Article Twelve: Rick Foster's Arrest

He threw about $100,000 in cash into the trunk of his 550 Mercedes Benz and fled the scene. He ended up at the David Williams Hotel in Miami and checked into the penthouse. Rick had never snorted cocaine before that day, but along with the $100,000, he threw a kilo of cocaine into his trunk—thus began Rick's first cocaine binge. Eddie went on to tell me what Rick had been doing for the past several days; wide awake and locked up in the penthouse of the David Williams Hotel.

Rick had not been to sleep for the past five days and was beginning to hallucinate. The Cockroach said that Rick needed to go to Stowe, Vermont so he could blend in with all the tourists and basically disappear. Rick's thought was that he could live in that town for the next several years and never be found by the authorities. My thought was that Rick was fearful of jail and didn't want to be arrested. But this was not the case; Rick was actually terrified of being killed by the mass-murdering drug dealer he was in business with (we'll call him Henry, his cocaine connection).

Rick's cocaine connection, Henry, was a major supplier in the United States and had lived in Miami since his immigration from Cuba in the mid-1950s. He was and always had been an extremely dangerous and violent man, basically a mass murderer.

Operation Court Broom ends with 2 judges guilty

Sun-Sentinel wire services

MIAMI — A massive corruption investigation involving Dade County judges and ex-judges accused of selling judicial favors ended on Monday with two judges found guilty of three counts of racketeering-conspiracy and extortion.

Two other judges were found innocent or jurors were deadlocked on the remaining 38 counts of money laundering, extortion, mail fraud and racketeering. Prosecutors said they plan to retry the judges on the deadlocked counts.

The investigation, dubbed Operation Court Broom, was the second largest judicial corruption inquiry in the United States, after Chicago's Operation Greylord, where 67 officials pleaded guilty and 15 judges were convicted.

On Monday, a federal jury of eight women and four men found suspended Dade County Judge Harvey Shenberg, 49, guilty of racketeering-conspiracy and one count of extortion. Former Circuit Judge David Goodhart, 63, was found guilty of racketeering-conspiracy.

Each count carries a maximum sentence of 20 years in prison. U.S. District Judge Jose Gonzalez set sentencing for July 1.

Lawyers for Goodhart and Shenberg said they would appeal.

The other two defendants, suspended Circuit Court Judge Phillip Davis and former Circuit Judge Alfonso Sepe, were either found innocent or the jurors were undecided on the charges.

Florida's biggest judicial corruption investigation in history, accused judges of taking bribes and fixing cases. The government's indictment accused the four judges of accepting the money in exchange for official acts, such as lowering bail, revealing the existence of arrest warrants, releasing confidential information, returning seized property and suppressing evidence.

Article Thirteen: Operation Court Broom

In the early 1980s, the Dade County Police launched an investigation named "Operation Court Broom." Operation Court Broom targeted the lawyers and judges who were selling confidential court room information to drug dealers before and during their criminal trials (see article thirteen). This would include the names and addresses of confidential informants who were key witnesses in major drug-trafficking trials. Basically, the witnesses would be killed and the drug dealers would go free due to a lack of evidence. The afore-mentioned lawyers and judges worked for Henry, among other major drug traffickers.

Rick was now a liability to Henry and could be used by law enforcement as a confidential informant (meaning, he could deal his way out of the trouble he was in). Therefore, Henry would not think twice about killing Rick, which would sever any connection between the two. Rick was not afraid of jail—Rick was afraid of Henry, and he realized that he'd be extremely vulnerable in jail and would have no way of protecting himself.

So it was clear to me, I needed to help my friend. The Cockroach also told me that someone had tried to drive Rick out of town a couple of days earlier but had failed miserably. They reached Palm Beach on I-95, and Rick got out of the car at a gas station and went in to make a call on the pay phone. After the call, Rick walked back to the car and forgot to pick up his brief case he had left at the pay phone. They realized their mistake about thirty minutes later and rushed back to the gas station, but it was closed (around four in the afternoon) and the pay phone was inside. They discovered later that the gas station owner had found the brief case containing about $40,000, some cocaine, and Rick's real and fake IDs, and had driven it to the local police station. Rick's driver turned the car around and returned to Miami. He was now back in the penthouse at the David Williams Hotel on his fifth day of no sleep. Hearing this terrible news about Rick, we picked up the phone and called him immediately. I told him I'd be at the hotel at nine tomorrow morning with a rental car and I'd drive him to Stowe, Vermont.

The next morning, I was at the hotel in the basement parking lot at about nine o'clock. I took the elevator up to the penthouse and knocked on the door. Rick was into his sixth day now of his first cocaine binge. I could hear him pacing back and forth and talking to himself in the room. I kept pounding on the door, and finally he let me in. Rick was a big guy, six feet seven and about 240 pounds. He was also the illegitimate son of Lionel Barrymore (the movie star), and he looked just like him. I grabbed his bags in one arm and Rick in the other arm, shoved him into elevator, and headed for the basement. We pulled out of the hotel at about ten that morning and headed for Vermont. Three days later, we'd be at the hotel in Stowe. During the trip, Rick told me why he had been so frightened; not of being jailed, but of Henry. Rick said that he and his partner had been buying kilos of cocaine from Henry for several years and driving them to Aspen, Colorado. They were not allowed to buy cocaine from anyone else if they bought from Henry; this was Henry's steadfast rule. About a couple of years earlier, Rick's partner started buying cocaine from a source other than Henry (Rick didn't know about this); when Henry found out about it, he killed Rick's partner. Rick told me that Henry had called him one night several months ago around midnight and told Rick to meet him at his partner's apartment. Rick said when he entered the apartment, he noticed that it was covered in blood. Henry was there, along with a couple of his associates (killers). Henry smiled and handed Rick his partner's $25,000 Rolex watch; it was also covered in blood. No other words were spoken. Rick left the apartment, and he never forgot the rule. Rick always wore the Rolex. He had it on his wrist when he told me this story.

We had been in Stowe for a few days when Rick learned that Henry had come by his girlfriend's apartment a couple of days earlier, looking for Rick. It seemed he wanted to discuss the details of the arrest warrant and wanted to know where Rick was. I immediately flew back to Miami and picked up Rick's girlfriend and brought her back up to Stowe. As long as Rick's location remained a secret, Henry could not hurt him; the only other person who knew where we were was the Cockroach.

I was due back at work in a couple of days when Rick asked me to stay on with him and remain in Stowe for a while. He said we could buy a bar and go into business together. Things in Miami were starting to get a little out of hand. I was breaking up with this girl I had been married to for a year or so, and she wasn't taking it very well. She had been vandalizing my car and sending crazy guys by the bar to beat me up. All in all, it was a good time to get out of Miami for a while. So, I said goodbye to Michael and Sheri and headed for Vermont.

I stayed in Vermont for about nine months; we were looking for a location to open a bar. I got there in April and made it all the way to December, till the snow began to fall. Having been born and raised in Miami, Vermont was way too cold for me. I was on the next plane back to Miami.

WORKING FOR GEORGE AND HANGING OUT WITH SHERI

When I got back to Miami in the winter of 1984, I moved in with a friend of mine, Ron. He had a two-bedroom apartment by Dadeland Mall, which doubled as a sportsbook in the afternoon. I started looking for a bar job, however there weren't any good bar jobs available at the time. So I hung out with my friends at the sportsbook in the afternoon and waited for a good bar job to surface.

Again, as fate would have it, Ron's partner in the sportsbook was Sheri's husband George. It seemed that while I was in Vermont, George had sold the movie company and the bar to cover his gambling debts;

George turned out to be a compulsive gambler. To fund his gambling habit, George also began selling cocaine and marijuana while running a sportsbook in the afternoon. Sheri was in no way happy with this situation; she had to get out of this marriage. She was not going to hit rock bottom due to George's problems. Sheri needed a profession, so in the summer of 1984, she started beauty school; she had always loved doing hair.

I was actually Sheri's first haircut; three hours to get my haircut and another hour to get it fixed by my friend Danny. I would go by Danny's salon after Sheri had cut my hair, and Danny would say, "You let her do this to you again? She must be beautiful!" I told him . . . she was. By the summer of 1985, Sheri had graduated from beauty school and was working at a salon in Coconut Grove. Her haircuts were looking really good by then; I didn't need Danny to fix them anymore.

Sheri separated from George in 1986 and filed for divorce in 1987; the divorce was final in 1988. I thought it best to not pursue Sheri till her divorce was final. Meanwhile, I was working for George (from 1984 to 1987), driving mostly marijuana and occasionally cocaine up to Pennsylvania while I was waiting for the bartending job market to grow. I'd make about $3,000 per trip, so I just kept on doing it. I felt comfortable driving on the highways with a trunk load of pot and coke. George was busy, so I was busy, and the next two years went by pretty quick. However, in February of 1987, I was arrested in the Carolinas for drug trafficking.

I had brought up from Miami two kilos of cocaine and had delivered it to one of our customers. A confidential informant had notified local police that a delivery of cocaine was coming in at a farm house in the Carolinas, so the police were waiting when I got there. I spent the next month in the holding facility waiting to be bonded out. I returned to Miami and immediately got a bartending job on Miami Beach while I waited for the outcome in the Carolinas.

The bar job I got on the beach was really cool. It was a Holiday Inn on the ocean that had been converted into a classic car hotel. It had a 1950s style bar in the basement and several bars in different locations around the hotel. I moved into a room at the hotel and worked the '50s bar at night and the tiki bar on the beach in the day time. Things were going pretty well, except for the pending charges in the Carolinas. They were moving pretty slow; we were able to keep postponing things.

A friend of mine at the hotel booked all the entertainment, so when a famous clairvoyant was scheduled, I wanted a private audience with him. I basically wanted to know if I was going to jail in the Carolinas and for how long. I was able to briefly speak with the psychic the night he came in. I asked him if I was going to jail in the Carolinas and he said an emphatic no. He also looked a bit strangely at me and said that he needed to speak with me after the show; it was important. I said okay, but I was too scared to go; I never met with him again. However, he did say that I wasn't going to have any problems in the Carolinas, but I didn't know how that could be. The police had seen me delivering the contraband to the farm house that night—but I was not in possession when they broke in.

I worked at the hotel for another few months, then moved to another bar in North Miami Beach, which turned out to be the best (money-wise) bar in which I had ever worked. The name of the bar was Hartigan's Pub, and it had an older, successful-type crowd. My personality fit in really good there, and I'd never made so much money. The bar had a 6 a.m. license, so we had a strong after-hours clientele. Everyone who worked in all the surrounding bars came by to drink with me at the end of their shifts; it was all bar people. It made for a very amusing and interesting night . . . every night.

There was one older Italian lady I really liked. Her husband had died a few years earlier; he had actually been a member of a local crime family there. She would come into the bar a couple of times a month with her body guards, and I would always clear a place off at the bar for her to sit, no matter how busy. Everyone at the bar liked her, so we all made her feel very welcomed whenever she came in. She was lonely without her husband, and making her feel welcomed at the bar really made her night. Whenever she left on a particular night, she would always tell me what a great time she'd had, and if I ever needed anything to please let her know. She was sort of our Godmother. I always thought that was a nice gesture on her part, but I was never really in need of anything—until one time.

The months went by at Hartigan's Pub, and we had been able to keep postponing the outcome in the Carolinas for almost a year now. However, in January of 1988, I was summoned back there to stand trial on drug-trafficking charges. Our plan was to go before the judge and ask for a public defender and see if we could postpone longer. The location in the Carolinas was a very small town with a court house in the center of the downtown area, just like in the old movies. It was actually quite scary—you really didn't know what they were capable of—but the judge agreed and assigned me a public defender. The only catch was that the judge wanted the trial to start the next day; it had all the makings of a kangaroo court.

My life flashed before my eyes. My new public defender, dressed in all black, smelling a little like gin, was going to run me through the Carolina legal system. However, he was also not happy with taking on a case he had to defend the next day; after all, he hardly knew my name. But he did have a plan: He asked me if I knew any doctors in Miami. He suggested I could actually fly back to Miami that afternoon, get a doctor's note that stated I had hurt my back, and call in sick for the upcoming trial. I thought he was kidding, but he was serious. (I could not fly back to the Carolinas with an injured back.)

I flew back to Miami and went out to find a doctor that would sign off on me having an injured back. This turned out to be a much harder task than I'd expected; even with all my connections, I could not find a doctor in Miami who would write a note stating I had an injured back. If I didn't have a doctor's note that said I couldn't fly to the Carolinas by the end of the day due to my injured back, I would have to fly back tomorrow and start my trial.

It was late in the afternoon, and I was driving around the streets of Miami trying to think of a solution; basically, I was out of ideas. Then all of a sudden, I remembered the older Italian lady from Hartigan's Pub; she'd always said if I need anything, just ask. I drove to her house in North Miami Beach and knocked on her door. She came to the door and was happy to see me. Then, realizing I might have a problem, asked me what was wrong. I was a little hesitant to ask; we all had made her feel so good at the bar, I didn't want her to feel bad if she couldn't help me. But she insisted, and I asked. She didn't say a word; she walked over to her telephone, spoke to someone, and told them I would be over there in five minutes to see the doctor. She turned to me and said, "Now get over there and get that note. I'll see you at the bar in a few days." She gave me a big hug and off I went.

I got my note and didn't have to go to trial the next day in the Carolinas. Actually, I never had to go back there for any trial—just like the clairvoyant predicted.

FEDERAL INDICTMENT SURFACES

I continued working at Hartigan's Pub, making lots of money and having lots of fun; however, in April of 1988, the federal government came calling, drug-trafficking indictments in hand; one for me and one for George. It seemed that the people in Pennsylvania had gotten arrested and charged with drug trafficking. They did not want to do the jail time, so they became government informants, and had informed on George and me. George sold the drugs and I drove them to Pennsylvania. Therefore, I was served a nine-count drug-trafficking indictment at my apartment in Miami and arrested. I bonded out later in the week. The federal system works differently than the state system; there are basically no postponements. We were set to go to trial in Philadelphia on the eighth of August, 1988, at 9 a.m.

GOOD BYE TO SHERI

Sheri came by my apartment the day before I left for Philadelphia and cut my hair. She was visibly upset; this was probably the last time I'd see Sheri for a long time. Actually, we were both upset. This would have been the perfect time to start a relationship with Sheri if I hadn't had to go to trial. She was free and single, and I was free and single—or maybe not so free. We knew we were probably going to lose our trial and get sentenced to at least five years (of which you serve thirty-four months). It was highly unlikely that Sheri would still be free and single three years from then, so any relationship we might have had, would probably never be.

The next day, I was on the plane to Philadelphia, leaving behind in Miami the only window of opportunity to have possibly had a life with Sheri. What that would have been like, we'd never know; my chance to be with my dream had passed.

So began our trial. George had a $100,000 attorney and I had a public defender. This is when I began to see that George was not going to live up to his end of the agreement. The agreement is, when you work for someone doing what I did, and don't make any mistakes that get you busted, your employer is supposed to pay all your legal defense costs and miscellaneous costs (i.e., lawyer, bond, hotel, food, etc.). I was looking at about 125 years of incarceration time, and this would basically be hinged on the expertise of my public defender. I was seeing my life flashing before my eyes . . . again.

Our trial took three weeks. We stayed at the Hilton in Cherry Hill, New Jersey, just over the river from Philly, during the trial. We were doomed from the start. The government had wire taps on George talking to the folks in Pennsylvania, explaining how he did business and how he made money. He was speaking like he had a license to deal drugs; there was no way we were not going to be convicted. On August 26, 1988, we were convicted on all counts and immediately incarcerated. Our sentencing hearing was scheduled for six months later. It seemed that the Philly Mafia trial of Nicky Scarfo and his seventeen associates was right behind ours on Judge Vann Antwerpen's (our federal court judge) calendar; we were going to have to wait till the end of the Scarfo trial to be sentenced.

We were all incarcerated together, George and I, and the Nicky Scarfo gang. Just to be sure no one bothered us in jail, Nicky Scarfo bought all the other inmates top-of-the-line Nike tennis shoes—about a thousand pairs of $150 Nikes. George and I are also Italian, so all the inmates figured that we were part of the Scarfo gang. Needless to say, we had no problems in the Philly jail while awaiting our sentencing.

I was still looking at 125 years for about six months. Every night when the Scarfo gang returned to the cell block, they would talk about what had gone on during their trial that day. They would also say how the judge was taking all this in and how it might affect my actual jail sentence. They said it could go either way. George and I were non-violent; there was no murder and mayhem involved in our trial. In contrast, there was nothing but murder and mayhem in the Scarfo trial; this made us look like good guys. The Scarfo guys would say that the judge might give us a leaner sentence because we weren't bad guys; however, it could go the other way. The Judge might be so saturated with criminals and criminal events that he locked us all up for a long time. The Scarfo guys would also say that the judge might take it easy on me, and just give me half of the 125 years (sixty years)—and then they'd laugh.

On August 26, 1988, in federal court, I was found guilty by jury to a nine-count indictment charging me with one count of conspiracy to distribute cocaine (count one); two counts of distribution of cocaine (counts five and seven); one count of conspiracy to distribute marijuana (count nine); two counts of distribution of marijuana (counts three and eight); and four counts of aiding and abetting (counts three, five, seven, and eight).

Six months later, I was sentenced to eleven years; five years of probation and six years incarcerated. This sentence meant that I would spend three years incarcerated (three years' credit for good time), and another ten years of probation/parole that would start after I was released. I was now on my way back to Florida to do my time at Eglin Air Force Base (AFB), a minimum-security federal prison camp.

LAST PHONE CALL TO SHERI

I called Sheri to let her know what sentence the judge had given me, and I could feel the sadness in her voice. I told her that I was on my way to Eglin AFB in North Florida, and she could come by and see me anytime; but I didn't want to push the request. I knew that Sheri cared about me, but she needed to get away from anyone with a checkered past. Sheri deserved the best, and I was hoping she would find it and lead a happy life. My life was ruined; a convicted felon, no profession, no way to earn an honest living—this was no life for Sheri. I was thinking I would never see her again, and that would probably be the best for both of us.

Sheri told me that she and a partner were opening a beauty salon called Getting It Off, in South Miami. I told her that I was really happy for her and wished her luck with her new business. I also told her I'd see her in a few years; however, I had no plans to ever see her again. I had been really close to achieving my dream, the girl I'd seen at Hunter's, but that, like other things in my life, had moved on past and left me behind. What lay in store for me was uncertainty at best, but I wasn't ready to give up yet. I would take what life had left for me and wring out all the (legal) opportunity I could find, and maybe then I might find some happiness in this lifetime. I thought, *You never know, maybe I might find Sheri again.*

CHAPTER 3
COMING OUT OF THE STORM

They call them Greyhound busses because, like a dog, they stop at each tall blade of grass (to pee). Greyhound busses are notorious for making many stops, in many small towns, to pick up passengers.

We'd picked up several passengers in the past few hours since our stop at the diner. Each time the bus reached max speed, it was only for a short time. The driver applied the break and we slowed down and stopped at the next bus station. Our journey continued to drag on.

They say that every dark cloud has a silver lining, and that you just have to go through all the darkness to get to it. As my thoughts drifted back to the federal prison camp on Eglin AFB, I began to see a silver lining starting to emerge.

EGLIN AIR FORCE BASE— FEDERAL PRISON CAMP

Eglin is the largest (area-wise) AFB in the military. It's located in the westernmost portion of the Florida panhandle, on the Gulf of Mexico. The prison camp is a collection of single-story dormitories, an athletic field, hospital, cafeteria, and gymnasium, located near the center of the base. My first job at Eglin was to cut the grass in and around the areas of the

US Army Ranger Camp. The Ranger Camp was located about forty-five minutes out from the center of the air force base. Army Ranger recruits would spend a few months at each air force base's Ranger Camp around the country to complete their training; Rangers are the best of the best.

I worked with four other inmates. Our job was to keep the grounds around the Ranger Camp dormitories groomed by maintaining the grass. I took my job very seriously. I felt that it was my duty to make this environment as pleasant as possible for the Ranger recruits; after all, they were giving all they had to protect our country. I really admired these guys and sort of wished I could become an Army Ranger. But that opportunity, like Sheri, had moved past and would never be a reality.

However, nothing was stopping me from making their environment look as good as possible. I expanded on my required duties to several acres of grass around the entire camp area. However, some of my fellow inmates who were working with me were not pleased; while they were doing as least as possible, I was doing as much as I could to make the grounds look good. This led to a physical altercation with one of them. I didn't start the fight; however, I did finish it. My coworkers never bothered me again.

Ultimately, it took all week to make the grounds look good using a tractor and bush hog, lawn mower, and weed eater. I would finish up every Friday and scan the area to be sure it looked good enough for my liking, only to return the following Monday to start over again. The grass in the North Florida heat (greater than ninety-five degrees) grows very fast. This went on through the first summer. My perseverance in cutting acres of grass in the blazing North Florida heat (while making the Ranger Camp look good) did not go unnoticed.

The civilian employee who managed the maintenance in and around the Ranger Camp called me into his office one afternoon. His name was Mr. Hobbs and he looked like a character right out of the Paul Newman movie *Cool Hand Luke*. He looked like one of the South Georgia prison guards, and he looked pretty aggravated about something. He told me to grab a donut and a Coca-Cola and sit on the couch; he wanted to talk to me about something. First of all, inmates were not allowed to eat or drink anything given to us by anyone. So when I hesitated before grabbing a donut and a Coke, he glared at me and said, "Just take them. You're working hard out there!" So I did.

Mr. Hobbs went on to tell me that my stay at the prison camp was just a "small portion of [my] life" and that I "want to leave with everything [I] came with." He said, "That grass isn't going anywhere"; that no one expected me to work as hard as I was working. "Just slow down, do a fair day's work, and one day someone will give you a bus ticket and a hundred dollars and send you back home. You're making the Ranger Camp look really good and we appreciate it; however, we're worried about you working too hard in this North Florida heat."

I couldn't believe my ears. North Florida folks really don't like South Florida folks; and I was a South Florida drug dealer; he should really not have liked me. He should really have been treating me like a slave or something. However, he was legitimately concerned about my health, and basically wanted to protect me from my overenthusiastic self. I thanked him for the refreshments and assured him that I would slow down and basically work like a normal human; however, I never did. I just made it look like I was moving slower.

After several months passed, a couple of fellow inmates (to whom I taught weight training) became concerned with my apparent weight loss and constant exposure to the sun. One of the inmates had been involved in my case, and the other had been convicted of illegal political lobbying. The latter was due to be released in a month and wanted me to take over his job as fire-alarm installer on the air force base. This would develop into one of the best opportunities of my life; the silver lining surrounding my dark cloud was beginning to show.

I didn't act on this offer right away. I was concerned about my grass. Also, the prison camp didn't like to shift inmates from one job to another. However, after much prodding by my inmate friends, I finally went to see (Ranger Camp) Master Sergeant Littlejohn to see if he would release me to a different job. These Rangers are pretty tough, and I didn't think he'd like being bothered by some inmate with a request. I walked into his office; he looked up and smiled and said, "Larry, what can I do for you?" I explained that I had an opportunity to work at a vocational job that I could ultimately do after my release. He asked if this was good for me. I responded yes, and he said, "Then I want you to do it, and I wish you all the best after your release." He said that I had made the camp look really good over the past several months and they had really appreciated it. This was when I came to realize that hard work overcomes a lot.

The following week, I started working for Carlos Duncan (a civilian employee supervised by Harold Owens) carrying a ladder and toolbox, while responding to fire-alarm repair calls on Eglin Air Force Base. Carlos would ask for a certain tool while installing or repairing a fire alarm panel, and I would retrieve it from the toolbox and hand it to him. As I watched and learned, I began to hand Carlos the correct tool before he would ask for it. As time passed, Carlos had me working on my own, installing and repairing fire-alarm panels and erecting antennas. Harold Owens (a manager and civilian employee) also had me attend electronics classes to increase my knowledge of electricity. As time progressed, I began to see that Harold Owens had taken an interest in my development as an electronics technician. Harold had placed me into the world of electronics and was personally making sure I was taught and I understood DC/AC electronics. He was allowing me to develop a skill set that I could potentially use after my release, which could lead to an honest and productive life. Because he managed the EMC group (fire-alarm repair), all the other civilian and military employees also aided in making me the best technician I could be.

How I migrated into the world of electronics can be directly attributed to Harold Owens and the guys in the shop; my development was a group effort. Just prior to my release, Harold set up a fire-alarm installation position for me at Homestead Air Force Base by communicating with his equivalent in Homestead; however, this position would only be available after my release from the halfway house.

What Harold Owens and the guys at the shop had done was give me hope—and "hope" is defined as an "optimistic state of mind that is based on an expectation of positive outcomes with respect to events and circumstances in one's life."

I continued to work for Harold and the guys till my release in June of 1990. The guys gave me a going-away party (cake, pizza, and all) and sent me back out into the world to prosper. See the pics below.

Picture Six: Eglin Air Force Base EMC Shop—My Going-Away Party

Picture Seven: Harold Owens, Civilian Employee Shop Supervisor

Picture Eight: My Cake

Picture Nine: The Cake—Just Say No Next Time

Picture Ten: Bon Voyage

A couple of weeks after my release, Harold sent me a letter. In the letter was some information on the job at Homestead Air Force Base (AFB), some advice about starting back to school and what courses to take, and a prayer to recite. Harold wrote that the Homestead job might happen, but it wouldn't open up for the next several months. He also advised me to take an introduction-to-algebra course, and an AC/DC electric course while I was waiting for the job to open-up; this would help me get the job at Homestead AFB. Harold also wrote me a prayer to say six times a day for nine days. He said if I did this, things I wanted to happen in my life would begin to happen. I recited the prayer six times each day for the next ten years.

Skip How's Every Thing going. Sorry I've Taken So long getting Back in Touch with you. We Sure Miss you in The shop But we are glad you are out and getting with it.

I Just Talked To Dan Long and he told me That They have gotten about 4 Big Jobs out For Bid and if They Get any one of them They will Put you To Work.

So Hang in There and be PaTient and Trust in The Lord and Things Will Break For you. Don't get Discouraged if Things Seem To happen Slow (Slower is Better). Remember you have a Lot of Friends up here and if you Need any help all you got To do is Let Some one Know. My Mailing Adress is P.O. Box 152 Valpariso Fla. 32580 My home Phone is (904) 729-1316 if I Can help you in Any Way Just LeT Me Know.

P.S. Say This Prayer 6 Times a Day For Nine Days and Things That you Want To happen Will start happening For you.
May The Sacred Heart of Jesus Be praised, Adored and Glorified, Through out The World For ever and Ever, Amen.

your Friend
Harold Owens

Picture Eleven: Harold's Letter and Prayer (in the Blue Box)

CHAPTER 4

HOPE, CONFIDENCE, AND DETERMINATION TAKES A HAND

BACK IN THE BUS; ARRIVING IN MIAMI

During my confinement, I realized early on that to recover the lost years of my life an extreme amount of hard work would be needed. By "lost years of my life," I mean the years leading up to and including the years of confinement; therefore, upon my release at age forty, time would be a critical factor. So, to enhance my physical capacity, I increased my strength and endurance by exercising with weights and running six days a week. To enhance my mental capacity, I completed several classes on small engine repair and outboard motor repair (taught at the prison), and computer literacy (taught at the community college). In my eyes, I had completed everything I could do to prepare myself for release.

However, somewhere along the line, during the past few years in federal custody, I felt like I had somehow regained my inner strength. I first started having these feelings when I got to the Ranger Camp at Eglin. I felt like I had a "purpose" again; I felt driven to succeed, steadfast in my desire to make something out of my failed life.

But, as the bus converged on my stop in Miami, fear stared me in the face. Being arrested by the FBI, losing our jury trial and being convicted on all nine counts of our indictment, spending the next few years incarcerated in federal prison—nothing was more fearful than, at age forty, stepping off the bus in Miami. I had no career. I had no money. I had no relationship. I stood there in the early morning hours looking into the abyss, thinking I had no future.

However, something in me had changed, and I began to realize it during the bus ride back to Miami. Mulling over my life and connecting all the dots, I began to clearly see who I was and what I needed to accomplish—. I was confident, focused, and determined to control the outcome of my life.

THE HALF WAY HOUSE

The bus dropped me off on US 1 in downtown Miami. It was five in the morning and there was no one around. I caught a cab and proceeded to the halfway house. Upon reaching the halfway house in the early morning hours, my first day was consumed with obtaining a driver's license, insurance, employment, and a class schedule from the community college. Harold Owens had advised me to take an electronics and math course in preparation for the job at Homestead AFB. I also discovered that the Pell Grant was available, and that the US government would pay my college tuition. So, the following Monday I began a full-time job installing fire sprinklers, and also began the fall semester at Broward Community College, taking DC electronics and algebra courses.

By the end of my six-month term at the halfway house, I had earned an A in both classes at the community college; had been offered a permanent position installing fire sprinklers by the Union; and had a pending fire-alarm-installation position at Homestead AFB. After weighing all my options, I decided to move back in with my parents and enhance my education by pursuing an associate of science degree at Miami Dade Community College. This degree would allow me to enter the workforce as a professional technician in the electronics field. In January of 1991, as my federal supervision program began, I started classes at Miami Dade Community College, along with a part-time job making key lime pies at Pie Are Round, Inc.

It seemed that Billy and Joe (who had previously owned Zackery's bar) had gotten out of the bar business and started a key-lime-pie manufacturing business. Due to my parole requirements, I needed to work several hours a week, along with attending school; this job worked well.

SHERI ON MY MIND

As I geared up for the next couple of years at Miami Dade Community College, I couldn't help but think about Sheri. I hadn't been in contact with her since our last call in Philadelphia, when I told her about my sentence. Complicating Sheri's life by trying to be a part of it was something I still did not want to do. I still felt that Sheri needed to distance herself from anyone with a checkered past—including me. She deserved the best, and I was hoping she had found it while I was away.

I had made some personal gains while at Eglin Air Force Base working for Harold and the guys and was on a path to obtaining an associate of science degree at Miami-Dade Community College. There was still a bit of uncertainty in my life, but not as much as when I'd last spoken with Sheri. I was really concerned about my future at this point and needed to focus all my attention on my studies. I was thinking perhaps I would touch base with Sheri after I got a little further down the road with my school stuff.

My days were filled with going to school, studying, working out in the gym, and making key lime pies. I wanted to be in good shape just in case I did have the opportunity to see Sheri again.

MIAMI DADE COMMUNIT Y COLLEGE

School was very difficult for me; I was taking advanced math classes, electronics classes, studying ten hours a day, and making As'. In January of 1992, I was advised by my Uncle Bud to seek a bachelor's degree in electrical engineering due to my excellent grades and GPA. I talked it over with Dr. Gary Goldapple (my government-provided psychologist), and he also agreed that earning a bachelor's degree would be fantastic.

Dr. Goldapple was the psychologist I'd been ordered to see for several months as part of my federal release program. He was very excited about my choice to further my education and advised me to seek out the highest rated engineering institutions and apply to them. I applied to Florida International University in Miami, the Florida Institute of Technology in Melbourne, University of Florida in Gainesville, and Georgia Tech in Atlanta. After several months, I was notified of my acceptance to each institution that I had applied. However, my first choice was the Georgia Institute of Technology (Georgia Tech) in Atlanta.

I still hadn't touched base with Sheri since my release. I was scared to death about what I was going to do with the rest of my life, so I stayed extremely focused on my studies and working out at the gym. I was thinking that I'd contact her after I got going at Georgia Tech.

GEORGIA TECH

I began Georgia Tech's College of Electrical and Computer Engineering full time in the fall of 1992, at the age of forty-one. The school was incredibly difficult; I was attending classes and studying in excess of twenty hours a day (every day) and just making Cs and an occasional B. I was competing against the brightest and most talented individuals in the nation, and at this pace, failure seemed imminent; however, quitting was never an option.

I remembered speaking with my friend Dave, a University of Miami professor, and telling him I was leaving for Atlanta to attend Georgia Tech. Dave asked me if I had lost my mind. He explained that Georgia Tech was extremely difficult—"It's nothing like Miami Dade Community College." However, this was my last chance at accomplishment. This was my last chance to be something. This was my last chance to turn failure around. This could also be my last chance to see Sheri again. If I could somehow make it through this institution and earn a bachelor's degree in electrical engineering, then I would have a future and something tangible to bring to a relationship with a girl like my Sheri.

As the year's ticked by, the uncertainty that predicted the outcome of my life was ebbing away and being replaced with confidence. As I said when I got to Eglin AFB to begin my prison sentence, I was not ready to give up yet, and I would wring out all the opportunity in life I could find and strive for success.

Now, there I stood on the steps of one of the most prestigious engineering schools in the country, a member of its student body. Two short years earlier I was stepping off a Greyhound bus with nothing more than a pulse. I'm convinced that the confidence that replaced the uncertainty in my life would allow me to persevere. *And yes*, I thought, *you never do know. I might still have a chance with Sheri again.*

Yes, my friend Dave was correct. Georgia Tech was incredibly difficult. As I worked and pushed forward in very small increments I thought back to the grass at the Ranger Camp. I remembered pushing a mower in the blazing heat of the North Florida summer down acres of rows of grass, determined to complete the entire job by the end of each week. I remembered experiencing satisfaction as I looked over a beautifully manicured lawn at the end of the day on each Friday, only to start over again the following Monday. I remembered starting at the top of a long row of grass completely fatigued and then pushing through to the end of the row, fully expecting never to make it, but after reaching the end, actually ready to mow another row. I used that mindset to push through the quarters at Georgia Tech, row by row or class by class as the years slowly moved past.

After one and a half grueling years at Tech, opportunity first surfaced in the form of a transistor class taught by Dr. Martin A. Brooke in the fall quarter of 1993. He gave us a design project due at the end of the quarter, and also gave us some suggestions as to what designs to use. I had developed an excellent work ethic while at Tech, however my grades didn't represent my efforts. Test-taking was not my strong point; I understood the material, but my thought process was slow. In contrast, a design project is different; I can work long and hard creating a quality design that *does* represent my efforts.

I handed in my project on time at the end of the fall quarter. I thought it looked really good. I wouldn't know *how* good till the beginning of the winter quarter, after returning from the three-week Christmas break . . . after reuniting with Sheri!

SHERI'S BACK IN MY LIFE

Finals were completed, the fall quarter was done, and I was still in the game at Georgia Tech. It was time to go back home to Miami and relax for the next three weeks. I flew out that night and moved back into my parents' house for the month. First thing I did the following morning was go to the gym and work out. All my old friends were at the gym; I had been working out there since 1968, when I was sixteen years old—I was now forty-two. My old friends had followed me through all the gains and pitfalls of my life. They were all glad to see me and glad to see I was doing well at Georgia Tech, excited about my new career.

I was doing chest exercises that day, just finishing up my bench presses, when Mike E. walked in the gym. I had known Mike for many years and he was happy to see me. He was also doing chest exercises that day and asked if he could join me, and I said sure. I did a set, then he did a set, then I did another set, and he'd started to do another set, when he looked at me and asked, "Do you know a girl named Sheri?" My heart stopped again. (The first time was when I saw Sheri at Hunter's Bar, then at Rainbows.)

Mike said that he'd been at Sheri's salon a week or so ago and Sheri was asking him about me. She wanted to know if he had seen me and what was I doing. Mike told me that Sheri wanted me to call her. I told him I would when he and I finished working out. Mike finished his set, then sprang off the bench and said, "No! You need to call her right now!" Mike pulled me over to the pay phone and called Sheri.

My mind was racing. The last time I'd spoken with Sheri was just after I'd been sentenced. All the thoughts I had about staying away from Sheri for her own good didn't apply anymore. I was an up-and-coming Georgia Tech electrical engineering student with a bright future. I was free and single at the time, but was Sheri free and single? What would be the chances of that? Also, there were no criminal indictments standing in the way, which was a plus on my end. It was a long shot, but I knew one thing: I was about to speak on the phone with the girl I'd been in love with since 1977.

Mike got Sheri on the line and handed me the phone. Sheri said, "Where are you?" I told her I was at the gym working out with Mike E.. She told me to come to her salon right now; I told her I had to finish my benches first. Then she said that they were having a Christmas party at the salon that night, and asked if I could be there at seven o'clock . . . I was there at seven.

When I arrived, Sheri was in the bathroom changing her clothes for the party. As I waited, my thoughts went back to Hunter's and Sheri screaming at me over the bar, then to Rainbows and drinking with Michael Taylor, and then (how could I forget?) the terrible haircuts she would give me when she was in beauty school (and Danny saying, "This girl must be gorgeous"—and he was right).

I was waiting for her to come out of the bathroom. Mike had said that she'd gained some weight, so I really didn't know what to expect. Finally, Sheri emerged from the bathroom.

Sheri looked gorgeous (Mike was joking about the weight). It was great to see her! This was the first time we'd both been free from relationships at the same time, ever. We gazed into each other's eyes and spent the next three weeks together. (KF)

After being with Sheri, I began to realize that I had returned to caring about my future and how I would live the remainder of my life. I had felt like that before the terrible experience with "my city" left me emotionally empty, not caring about anything but the next day. Sometime during the last fifteen lost years, I had managed to find my way back to being me.

I think the time I spent in federal custody did so much more for me than I ever thought. Was it the time I spent with Harold Owens and the crew at Eglin AFB, their caring and direction made me see my self-worth and gave me hope? Or was it at Otisville Federal Prison in upstate New York, where the average sentence per inmate was fifteen years?

The prison actually looked like a Holiday Inn with concertina wire. The inmate population (eight hundred or so guys) was made up of Mafia wise guys and career criminals. These guys were extremely serious about what they did, and nothing was going to change them. This was their livelihood and jail was just a hazard of the job you'd like to avoid; however, if you found yourself there, you would make the best of it. I believe these guys understood their purpose and nothing or no one was going to sway them from it.

I think there's a lot to be said for understanding your purpose and staying the course. I'm not trying to glorify the criminal element in the Otisville Federal Prison, I'm saying that not allowing someone or something to emotionally push you off track to benefit their end is a trait I lacked. I basically allowed "my city's" Police Department to push me off track and take from me my passion in life, which, at the time, was law enforcement. This left me feeling empty of purpose and floundering in life. I believe I lost fifteen years of my life trying to overcome this attack.

I always knew who I was, but I was pushed off track, swayed by a terrible life experience. I was back now, and nothing was going to stop me from my purpose or excelling in life. I would work. I would per-se-vere. I would become a respected individual. Success would be the re-sult. I had chosen electrical engineering at Georgia Tech to endure.

After three weeks with Sheri, I knew that I wanted to spend the rest of my life with her. I felt pride in knowing that together we could create a beautiful life, and that I could hold up my end.

When I stepped foot back in Miami, returning on the Bus Ride Back, I stepped off as the man I always was: I had hope, I knew my purpose, and I had the drive to reach it. The only thing missing was Sheri, and I was going to ask for her hand in marriage.

RETURNING TO GEORGIA TECH WITH SHERI

So, after handing in my design project at the end of the quarter, Dr. Brooke stated that my design was the best he had ever seen, and subsequently offered me a research assistant position in his analog group, starting the winter quarter of 1994. This was an extremely prestigious position! At the time, research assistants were mainly graduate and PhD students; as a second-year undergraduate, this appointment was very flattering.

Not realizing at first the magnitude of what Dr. Brooke was offering, I was concerned about how Sheri was going to deal with this. We set a date to be married in March of 1994 (three months later); Sheri was going to sell her part of the salon in Miami and relocate to Atlanta. I was spending most all my waking hours in school and studying, so I was concerned about not having enough time for Sheri.

I called her to ask what she thought we should do about Dr. Brooke's offer. I would be so busy working for him and attending classes that we wouldn't have time to go to the movies or anything. Sheri's reply was "I have already been to the movies! Tell that man you will accept his offer. This could be really good for us!" We accepted Dr. Brooke's offer and I went to work for him as a research assistant, and we were married April 16, 1994 in Helen, Georgia at a bed and breakfast.

A couple of months after I started with Dr. Brooke, he had a party at his house. All the Ph.D and grad students who worked for him were there, along with several other Georgia Tech professors and some of their students. At one point during the party, Dr. Brooke took Sheri and I aside and talked to us about our choice of career paths and his feeling on the subject. He said that my choice of analog IC design was a very good one, and that after graduation I should have no problem securing a well-paying job in that field.

Most all of Dr. Brooke's students who worked for him were focused on analog IC design. However, Sheri and I didn't know exactly what analog IC design was, but we looked at each other and said yes. We thought long and hard on the subject and decided to move in that direction. Later, we left the party and drove home. Sheri asked me what analog IC design was and I really didn't know exactly. When we got back home, I pulled out every book in my office, trying to nail down what exactly was analog IC design.

BACHELOR'S DEGREE GRADUATION FROM GEORGIA TECH

Eventually, I figured out exactly what analog IC design was, because in June of 1995 (at the age of forty-four) I graduated from Georgia Tech, earning a bachelor's degree in electrical and computer engineering. I was also published in several articles that were written on the work I did as a research assistant for Dr. Brooke.

We had a small party to celebrate our graduation, and in attendance were my parents, my dad's two brothers, and my mom's mother. One of my dad's brother's, my Uncle Sammy, had graduated from Georgia Tech the year I was born, in 1951, earning a bachelor's degree in electrical engineering. My Uncle Sammy loved his school and had stayed active in activities and donations all his life. I remember when I called him up to discuss the possibilities of me attending Georgia Tech. This conversation could have gone a lot of different ways. I wasn't exactly the poster child of a Georgia Tech student, with all my felony convictions and other nonsense I had amassed over the years. However, I had spent the last two years at Miami Dade Community College earning straight As in every class (approximately 60 credit hours). But there I was, asking Uncle Sam for basically a recommendation to attend his pride-and-joy school.

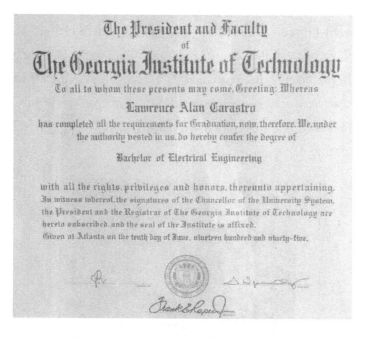

Picture Twelve: Bachelor's Degree in Electrical Engineering Diploma

When I got him on the phone, he asked, "What can I do for you?" My Uncle Sammy was a man of few words. I held my breath and said that I wanted to continue my education at Georgia Tech, and my thought was to earn a bachelor's degree in electrical engineering. My Uncle Sam could have said a lot of different things to me, all of them unflattering, and he would have been right. However, all he said was "When do you want to start?" I told him in the fall, which was several months away.

I began the rigors of Georgia Tech in the fall of 1992. Sheri came up to Atlanta to join me in 1994, and together we pushed through to graduation as husband and wife. Uncle Sammy and Aunt Gloria would come up every year and take Sheri and I to dinner at the finest restaurants in Atlanta; they were checking on us to be sure we were doing okay. Uncle Sammy passed away in 2006 at the age of seventy-eight. He had suffered from multiple sclerosis for most of his life, but he never let it impede his actions or desires. Uncle Sam had founded Carastro and Associates Engineering Firm in Tampa, Florida in 1960 and it thrives to this day, managed by his son and Georgia Tech grad, Paul Carastro. Uncle Sam was a retired full bird colonel in the US Air Force Reserves, and he and his wife Gloria also set up a scholarship fund for students at Georgia Tech.

Picture Thirteen: My Uncle Sam

Uncle Sammy and Aunt Gloria were both very proud of Sheri and I when we earned our bachelor's degree that day.

Sheri and I continued our studies at Georgia Tech. While working for Dr. Brooke, I was able to bring up my GPA to 3.0, which allowed me to enter the master's program at Tech. I graduated again from Georgia Tech in June of 1997 at the age of forty-six, earning a master of science degree in electrical and computer engineering. I added several more publications to my resume, which were also written on the work I did as a research assistant for Dr. Brooke.

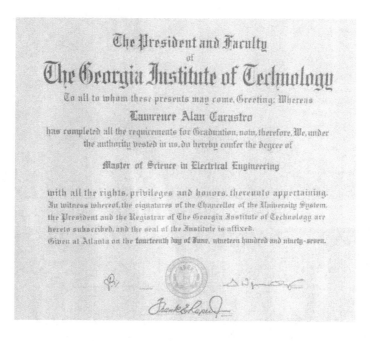

Picture Fourteen: Master of Science in Electrical Engineering Diploma

Meanwhile, Sheri had amassed a large clientele base working as a hair stylist. We had an opportunity to lease space in a shopping center and decided to open Sheri's second beauty salon. After attending school for the past seven years, I took my first summer off to buildout the salon. Sheri had put me through engineering school, so there was no question that my first engineering project would be her salon. However, I wasn't really a builder; the only screwdriver I knew was a vodka and orange juice.

I did my best, which turned out to be okay; I'd learned more than I realized at Georgia Tech. The salon took ten weeks to build and was a success for nineteen years. The before and after pictures are below. Sheri and I work very well together as a team!

Original Condition of Lease Space

The Finished Product

Picture Fifteen: Original versus Finished Salon Lease Space

In December of 1997, Dr. Brooke asked if I would continue my education and start working towards a PhD degree. One of the big hurdles in the PhD program is the preliminary doctorate exam, and I had already taken the test twice, having scored eighteen out of a hundred and twelve out of a hundred (failing scores). Dr. Brooke encouraged me to take the test once more; this would be my final chance to enter the PhD program.

The next date for the preliminary doctorate exam was April 1998. To study for the test, I audited four classes (completing all homework assignments and tests) and studied old preliminary doctorate exam problems. I worked for the next four months in excess of fifteen hours a day to prepare for my last attempt at the PhD program.

As I stated previously, I had never been able to take tests well at Tech, which was because I always used memorization when learning new material. This method of learning worked well at Miami Dade Community College, where you were basically tested on the homework; however, at Tech, you were tested on the theory of the material and how it was applied to examples not given in the homework. Learning by memorization is inefficient and time-consuming in contrast to learning the theory of the material. To pass the preliminary doctorate exam I would have to completely change my learning scheme.

In April of 1998 I passed the preliminary doctorate exam, scoring in the high nineties out of a hundred. This was the best test I had ever taken; I was not only prepared but knew the scope of the material by theory.

For the next four years, Sheri and I pushed through the rigors of Georgia Tech's PhD program. I finished all my remaining electrical engineering classes while earning a minor degree in mathematics.

I'd come a long way in the field of mathematics. My math skills had been so weak when I started back to school at Miami Dade Community College that my first two algebra courses were "no credit" classes; I basically started with ninth-grade algebra. I finally started earning college credits after the third algebra class. I moved through complex algebra, trigonometry, pre-calculus, calculus one through five, differential equations, linear algebra, and some higher order math-function classes. All total, I took twenty-three math classes—I now had a math degree.

I was also doing research for Dr. Brooke as I was finishing up my PhD courses. Companies would come to Georgia Tech and pay to have the PhD students work on complex issues they face in the real world. My major field of study was analog circuit design (in contrast to digital circuit design). I design these transistor-based analog circuits on silicon substrates which are extremely small (see picture sixteen).

My first project was a "bi-directional fiber link"; Ford Motor Company was replacing all the copper wire in the engines of its vehicles with one optical cable. The integrated circuit chip (interface chip in picture sixteen) we designed and fabricated was at either end of the optical cable and was the interface between the cable and the electronics in the vehicle. The device works like the remote control for your TV set. One of the interface chips would flash a digital signal using the "emitter" (on the face of the chip, which emits a digital flash), and the signal would be picked up by the "photo-detector" on the other end of the optical cable. The interface chip we developed went into production and into the vehicles in 2002. I worked on this project from the summer of 1994 through 1997.

Picture Sixteen: Ford Motor Auto-Link IC Chip (2mm x 2mm)

After finishing up on this project, I moved to my PhD research, which was "A Passive Device Modeling Methodology." I had mentioned to Sheri before we were married, I would be so busy we wouldn't be able to go to the movies, and Sheri replied, "I have already been to the movies." And she meant it! It turned out that I was working all hours of the day and night. Sheri would

73

make me my breakfast in the morning, pack me a lunch for the afternoon, and bring me my dinner at school at all hours of the day and night.

I remember when we bought our first house in 1997. It was a three-bedroom, two-bath home in the Georgia mountains. As we were moving in, we were deciding which bedroom we would use for my office. Sheri commented, "Wow, I don't have to be the room girl anymore." I wasn't quite sure what she was talking about.

For the past few years we had always lived in a one-bedroom apartment to save money. She explained to me that my office had always been in the living room of the apartment, and Sheri had always stayed in the bedroom to read and watch TV; she never wanted to disturb my studying. I never realized this till then. I was really glad she didn't have to be the room girl ever again.

All through my years of education Sheri did nothing but sacrifice! She worked at her salon six days a week (ten to twelve-hour days) to support us through the school years. I was working for Dr. Brooke and earning a small stipend, which basically paid for my tuition at school and some other monthly bills. When Sheri lived in Miami before we were married she only shopped at the highest-end stores (Nordstrom's, Sacks, etc.). As we moved through our school years, Sheri shopped at Walmart and Target.

After we were married in April of 1994, our honeymoon consisted of us going back to our apartment and me studying for a lab final. Our first vacation was in 1999; I was presenting my PhD research at a conference in Las Vegas. My flight, the room at Caesar's Palace, and my meals, were all paid for by Georgia Tech, and we used some of our savings to have a great time in Las Vegas, and later when we drove to San Francisco, California.

However, when we arrived at Caesar's, our room wasn't ready yet, so we walked around in the casino. Sheri walked through some of the clothing shops, and I walked over to the poker slots. Back in the old days whenever I went to Vegas or Atlantic City (back then, the only places to gamble), I would peruse the poker slots to see if I could feel any "divine intervention" that would tell me a particular poker slot was ready to make a payoff. I had sort of good luck with this methodology, but it had been several years since I had used it.

I proceeded to wander through the casino in search of a specific poker slot on the verge of a payoff. After twenty or thirty minutes, I actually thought I may have found one. It was a quarter machine that would pay off $1,000 for a royal straight flush if you used four quarters. In the old days, I only played the dollar or five-dollar poker slots, and their payoffs were $10,000 and $20,000 for a royal flush (i.e., ace, king, queen, jack, ten of all the same suit). See picture seventeen.

We really didn't have a lot of money to gamble with, so I had to be frugal. That was something else I wasn't used to being. I started with one quarter and played a couple of hands. Then I said, what the heck, and started playing four quarters at a time. On my second set of four quarters and my first hand, I was dealt an ace, king, queen, jack, and three, all clubs. This was a flush—not a royal flush, but still a flush—that paid $200 on my dollar investment. I could have not asked for a second hand and just walked away with $200. However, I was sure this was divine intervention in process! I asked for one card on my second hand and got what you see below: a royal straight flush worth $1,000. Bells started ringing and lights started flashing and the attendant came over and handed me $1,000.

Sheri had heard all the commotion coming from where I was standing and walked out of the clothing shop and came over. She had told me earlier that she had seen a really nice outfit in one of the shops she liked but we didn't have the money to spend right now; we were on a budget. Well, the budget was gone. I handed Sheri a couple of hundred dollars for the outfit and we went on to spend a very enjoyable week in Las Vegas and San Francisco.

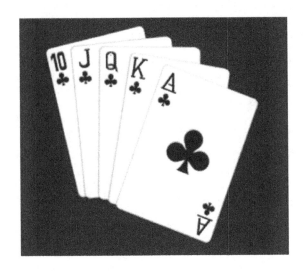

Picture Seventeen: A Royal Straight Flush

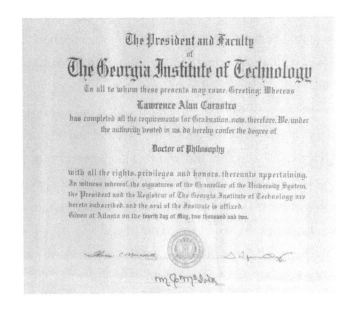

Picture Eighteen: Doctor of Philosophy in Electrical Engineering Diploma

I graduated in May of 2002 (at the age of 51 years old) from Georgia Tech, earning a Doctor of Philosophy in Electrical and Computer Engineering and became Dr. Brooke's eleventh PhD. graduate. Dr.

Brooke also won the Georgia Tech 2002 Institute award for Outstanding Thesis Adviser that year.

The graduation was held in the basketball arena at Georgia Tech. The graduates were seated on the court while the family and friends we seated in the elevated seats. While I sat waiting for my name to be called to receive my diploma, I was watching Sheri's reactions. One minute she was smiling and laughing, and the next minute she was crying—she was so excited! She had sacrificed so much to develop my career; no vacations, delivering my meals to the school at all hours of the day and night, and being the "room girl" for years at home. All her emotions were coming out. Sheri was so happy! After the graduation ceremony, we had a big party with all our friends from school and the salon. We even had Buzz, the Georgia Tech mascot, there (see the pics below). We were dancing to our favorite song, "After All" by Cher and Peter Cetera.

Picture Nineteen: Sheri and I at the PhD Party Dancing to Our
Favorite Song, "After All" by Cher and Peter Cetera

LAUNCH INDUSTRY CAREER

Prior to graduation in 2002, I began working for Phillips Semiconductors as a design engineer intern during the summer of 2000. My supervisor requested that I become familiar with a particular software tool, and to analyze at least one integrated circuit chip design (containing ten million transistors) during my three-month internship.

During that time period I became familiar with the tool and learned Unix shell scripting and several other programming languages to automate the software tool. Automating and optimizing the software tool ultimately located design errors missed by all other verification tools.

Basically, I found serious errors in several of their designs that they didn't know existed.

At the completion of my three-month internship, Phillips hired me full time in January of 2001. My responsibilities were increased to performing the abovementioned analysis on all IC chip designs completed by my office. As I further optimized the tool and refined the rendering and evaluation of the results, I began to analyze designs from other offices. Design engineers were having problems running the tool, and the results I generated far exceeded what the basic tool produced.

Assisting my coworkers, giving presentations at every opportunity, and researching the abovementioned analysis issues propelled me to expert within the company and team leader (in the abovementioned analysis) worldwide. I also published a paper on the above issues in the Phillips TCG newsletter, created a web page tutorial on how to run my scripts, and filed my first patent application on the software tool flow I created.

While working full time at Phillips Semiconductors, I was able to complete my PhD degree in May of 2002. My performance appraisal for 2001 and 2002, evaluated by my supervisor Mark T., highlights some of my strong points. The "Performance Against Key Areas of

Responsibility" category stated that I understood what it took to get the job done; was quick to learn CAD tools required to perform assigned tasks; went beyond the normal call to make a process run smoothly; and worked well with others and as a team member.

The "Personal Effectiveness in the Job" category listed my work performance as "far exceeding job requirements" at a stable rate, which is the highest in a list of five. These qualities propelled me from novice to expert within the company during a very short time span. As stated previously, all this was accomplished while completing my PhD degree. In September of 2002, Phillips closed my office (all coworkers were laid off); however, due to my critical competency I was offered a move package to any Phillips office in the United States. I chose Boston, Massachusetts, and was due to start there in January of 2003. During the second week of December 2002, due to the continued downturn in the economy, I was terminated due to a reduction in force. My last day with Phillips Semiconductors was December 31, 2002.

By the end of my employment with Phillips, my team was comprised of design groups from all over the world. I organized design handoffs, kept the designers up to date on analysis progress, developed and organized the results handoff, and worked with the design teams to evaluate results and correct design errors. However, one month later in February 2003, I was asked to travel to Eindhoven in the Netherlands (Phillips home office) to interview with Dr. Jos Gobbels about a research position. Due to the unsettled nature of being abroad (post-September 11), I declined the offer and instead took a one-year contract position in Dallas, Texas.

In summary, the learning years at Georgia Tech successfully propelled me into the world of electrical engineering. While at my first industry position at Phillips Semiconductors, I went from novice to seasoned professional in a very short time period. It was apparent Sheri and I had successfully made the leap from engineering school to the engineering workforce.

However, it was January of 2003, and due to the continued downturn in the electronics industry, finding the right position in Atlanta was going to be difficult. Atlanta was not a hot bed of opportunity for the particular skill sets I had, and the companies that were there weren't hiring at that point in time. I needed to reach out to other locations in the US, and to other companies that were hiring during this downturn.

DEFENSE DEPARTMENT WORK

In April of 2003 I began a one-year contract position with DRS Infrared Technologies (on the Texas Instruments campus) in Dallas, Texas. I was designing the analog circuitry for the next version of the night-vision equipment, and the laser radar for the Abrams tanks and Bradley fighting vehicles.

I actually felt like I had come full circle. I was back at the Army Ranger Camp; this time, instead of cutting grass, I was helping to keep our troops safe by designing more efficient electronic systems.

Sheri and I drove out to Dallas together and got me set up in an extended-stay-type hotel. Sheri and I were very close and the two of us being apart was going to be very hard on her. However, as usual, Sheri took it in stride and made the best of this terrible situation.

Sheri and I had been married now for about ten years, and as she was riding to the Dallas airport in the shuttle van to go back to Atlanta, she was in tears. I had to go to my new job that morning, so I hadn't seen how upset Sheri actually was. Being concerned, the shuttle driver tried to console Sheri. At one point he asked her how long we had been married, thinking by all the tears, we were newlyweds. Sheri said we'd been married for ten years. The driver responded, "Ten years?!" and they both started laughing. Sheri made it back to Atlanta okay, and I came home, and she came out to Dallas on as many weekends as we could possible afford. Thank God for cell phone headsets; it kept Sheri and I in constant contact. I think I talked to her more when I was away than when I was working in Atlanta.

TEACHING BACK IN ATLANTA
(DEAN OF THE SCHOOL)

The contract job lasted till December of that year. After its completion, I packed up my belongings and drove back to Atlanta. My friend Billy (who owned Zackery's and the key lime pies) was tired of living in Miami, so Sheri and I invited him up to stay with us in Atlanta for as long as he liked.

The lease space next to Sheri's salon in the shopping center was vacant, so we decided to expand our salon. Billy and I started the buildout in January of 2004 and would finish three months later. Meanwhile, I started looking for a job somewhere in the Atlanta area. Atlanta is the home of Georgia Tech, but does not have many electronic design-type jobs. The only position I could find was back at Georgia Tech working for one of my previous instructors. His name was Dr. Phil Allen and he was a world-class professor. This was a very prestigious position, and I was able to generate a conference paper from the innovated work we accomplished during that time.

To try and stay busy working in my field, I also took a teaching position with the University of Phoenix. The position was in Columbus, Georgia, about ninety miles from Atlanta, and I would drive there to teach a three-hour class two times a week. My students were non-traditional, meaning they were older and had been in the workforce for several years.

I really enjoyed teaching and facilitating the learning material to my students; from all accounts, they also enjoyed my class.

While I was teaching and working with Billy doing the salon buildout, I was also looking for a job more in my field. I couldn't find anything in Atlanta, but Harris Semiconductor in Melbourne, Florida, saw my resume and had me in for an interview. The position was a perfect fit; I would also be working with a guy I had graduated with from Georgia Tech. The hiring process was going well till we started talking about my federal felony convictions. I would need to have a top-secret security clearance to work at Harris; however a new law would prevent me from ever obtaining one. This was terrible news.

It seems that the "Smith Amendment," enacted in 2002, forbade anyone convicted of a felony from ever obtaining a security clearance. This was not only bad for me, but also bad for anyone presently holding a security clearance; losing a security clearance would cause a person to immediately lose their job. In 1997 when I was going to intern at Electromagnetic Sciences in Atlanta, they advised me that a felony conviction would not prohibit me from getting a security clearance; the Smith Amendment changed all that. While the Smith Amendment only impacted employees working on government projects, private industry was still wide open with opportunities. However, in 2008, the Smith Amendment was totally repealed. I can now hold a top-secret security clearance.

I continued on teaching for University of Phoenix and working on the buildout with Billy. A few months later, I was at Georgia Tech working on a project when I ran across Sidney. Sidney and I had graduated with our PhDs back in 2002 and had done research work together at Georgia Tech for several years. It seemed that Sidney and several of our colleagues had taken the research work we were doing, partnered with Georgia Tech, and created a startup company called Jacket Micro

Devices (JMD). Sidney had reached out to offer me a position, but was told that Sheri and I had moved to Boston with Phillips Semiconductors. I told him that Phillips had closed the office due to a reduction in force a week before we were due to move, and I was available for work. JMD had just secured more funding, so Sidney would be ready to hire me in a couple of months.

A couple of weeks after seeing Sidney, I got a call from one of the University of Phoenix directors; he wanted me to present the customer service presentation to all the University of Phoenix employees in Columbus, Georgia. Two days later, I was standing in front of about two hundred people singing the praises of good customer service, along with reciting numerous bar stories—all of which explained and showcased the value and importance of "good customer service." My presentation had gone very well; the University of Phoenix director called me the following day and offered me the position of dean of the school in Columbus, Georgia, and I accepted. I wasn't sure when Sidney's offer was going to come, and I had been out of full-time work for the past six months.

University of Phoenix sent me to Phoenix, Arizona for two weeks to train, then I returned to Atlanta to start my new position. As I got off the plane in Atlanta, Sidney called me and offered a senior RF design engineer position, starting immediately. I accepted, quit the University of Phoenix position, gave them the $2,000 they had paid me for my time and training (I felt bad about leaving), and headed off to work at Jacket Micro Devices. JMD would turn out to be the best job (career-wise) I have ever had!

JACKET MICRO DEVICES

My PhD thesis dealt with the circuit modeling of passive devices, which meant that I know how inductors, capacitors, and resistors behave in a circuit. The circuits I'd be designing at JMD were actually a type of circuit that I had never designed before. However, I attacked this problem like the grass at the Ranger Camp—keep moving and never stop!

I ramped-up into the job rather quickly; I started writing conference papers on the innovative circuits I was designing and was awarded one patent for a low-loss (high Q) inductor I designed. Little did I realize, the circuit design experience I was learning and perfecting would ultimately turn out to be very lucrative in my field.

As my career matured, I began to see that this type of circuit design was sought-after in the field, and not many engineers were proficient with this type of design. Therefore, my years at JMD had ultimately taught me a critical competency I would incorporate throughout my career. I worked at JMD for about five years; we ran out of funding and had to close our doors in 2009.

MY CAREER IN CALIFORNIA

I spent the next two years in Palo Alto, California, designing filters for satellite applications. Then I returned to Atlanta and worked for an electronic component manufacturer for a couple of years. This company had bought the rights to market the JMD technology from Georgia Tech; I was bringing up the technology within that company.

While I was in California, Sheri stayed behind in Atlanta running the beauty salon and growing the business. I had been hired full time with Space Systems Loral and they had given us a full move package; however, in 2009, 2010, and 2011, the real estate market was stagnant. We couldn't sell the house, so I would fly back to Atlanta every month or so and Sheri would fly out to California every month or so, for the next two years. Once again, thank God for cell phone headsets; we stayed in constant communication.

In 2011 I had an opportunity to return to Atlanta and bring up the JMD technology within the AVX corporation (large electronic component manufacturer). I hated to leave Space Systems Loral, but I had to get back to my Sheri; we missed each other terribly. The offer to work for AVX was very good, so I packed up and returned to Atlanta and my Sheri. I design electronic circuits, so I was able to work out of our house for the next two years. Sheri would finish up at the salon every night and I would be home waiting for her. It was great!

MY CAREER BACK IN FLORIDA, UP TO THE PRESENT

We did this for the next two years till a job offer came in to work for a company in Orlando, Florida. Once again, the job offer was very good, and we were very excited to be living back in Florida. However, this would mean that we'd be apart till we sold the house and the beauty salon in Atlanta. Sheri would spend three weeks out of every month in Atlanta working at the salon, then drive or fly to Orlando and spend one week out of every month with me and our animals.

This went on for the next three years, till we sold all our holding in Atlanta. During that time, however, Sheri felt that I might need more company at the house. We had our two kitties (Zazoo and Zoey), but we had seen this parrot at the pet store. His name was Zoolu and Sheri thought he would make a good addition to our family. Sheri also felt I might need some more company while she was in Atlanta. As seen in the picture below, Zoolu and I have intellectual conversations from time to time. These birds are very smart!

Picture Twenty: Zoolu, Our Parrot

In August of 2016, Sheri sold Salon Carastro in Atlanta so we could be together in Orlando. She'd had the salon for nineteen years and had amassed over four hundred clients; she was personally attached to each and every one of them. Sheri told me once that she always looked for that little kick in their step as the clients left the salon after having their hair done. If she didn't see that, then she would address it on their next visit, or she would call them and have them come back in for a touch-up or something.

After finishing a client's hair, Sheri would always look over her work as the client walked away to be sure it was to her satisfaction. I've also known Sheri to call a client back at the end of her day and have them come back in for a touch-up if she had seen something that was not up to her standards (even though the client was completely satisfied).

Sheri's passion is hair and making people as beautiful as they can be. Attending cutting classes, beauty seminars, trade shows, and any other vehicle at her disposal to keep her up to date with the latest technology in her field made Sheri the best stylist she could be. Fueled by her passion and capabilities, Sheri brings to reality her client's vision every time she steps behind her chair. I believe the satisfaction she extracted from this enabled her to endure the time we spent apart and made it all bearable.

Someone else in our life also helped Sheri fill the void of my absence; it was our niece, Lisa; we call her "Muffin." She was and is to this day very special to us; she's like our own daughter. She stayed with us in Atlanta through part of her high school and college years. Muffin managed the beauty salon and worked right along side her Aunt Sheri for several years; she was the perfect child. She has since returned to Miami and finished up her nursing degree and works as a registered nurse in the emergency room at a major hospital in Miami.

Muffin is just like her Aunt Sheri, extremely caring, cool in any situation, and thinks logically on her feet; she's a perfect fit for the high-stress dynamic environment of the ER. I've watched her at work. She wades through the fast-paced activity that only a big-city ER can deliver, and calmly deals with and solves any and all problems. She's amazing. She's our Muffin.

Saying good bye to all her clients during those last days at the salon was a sad time. The only thing worse than Sheri leaving was Sheri staying; I believe her clients felt that way. Her clients loved her, and they wanted us to be together, more than anything else, and I love them for that! Sheri and I cherish the time we had with all our clients and will always be there for them in whatever capacity that might be. Perhaps a better way to say goodbye is to say "au revoir."

Now we're both in Orlando, Florida. I'm working for an electronics company as a senior RF circuit design engineer, designing acoustic filters that go into hand-held mobile devices and high-power RF systems. I'm also working with a coworker, bringing up the JMD technology within the company, basically marrying acoustic and JMD technologies together. This is giving our company an innovative edge over our competition and is turning out to be very lucrative for the company.

For the past eighteen years, I've worked exhaustively to amass an extensive career in the electronics industry. I have two patents and six patent applications under review at the present time. I've also written more than fifteen conference papers and presented them at conferences all over the country.

Every goal Sheri and I have struggled for, we've accomplished, and sacrifices we've made together, have never felt like sacrifices because we've been together.

Starting with ninth-grade algebra and ending up with a mathematics degree. Starting as a bartender and ending up as a doctor of philosophy in electrical engineering. Walking off a Greyhound bus in the early morning hours with nothing more than hope and a desire and ending up with an electrical engineering career and a life I could have only imagined.

Just think, all this happiness was spawned from what would turn out to be the darkest days of my life.

CONCLUSION

GROWING UP

In 1961, when I was nine years old, we moved into our new house in Southwest Miami. Around the corner from the house, was a golf driving range, which at that age, fascinated me. One day I was exploring in the weed-covered vacant lot next to the driving range and found some golf balls. I had never seen a golf ball before and thought they looked really cool. As I was picking up the golf balls, I looked up and saw a 1957 T-Bird speeding towards me on the driving range grass. A man got out of the car and asked me why I was stealing his golf balls. I replied, "They are over here in the weeds. I didn't think they belonged to anyone." He answered, "No, they belong to me." We stood there for a moment looking at each other. I was afraid to move. This man had just caught me stealing his golf balls, and I thought I was in trouble. It turned out, I wasn't.

His name was Adam Adams and he was the head-pro and manager of the driving range. He said if I wanted to dig through the weeds and search for lost golf balls, then he would give me a bucket to put them in, and then I could hit them out for free at the driving range.

This event (at nine years old) would turn out to be a pivotal point in my life. I had started out the day with nothing to do and decided to explore my new surroundings. This led me to the vacant lot and finding lost golf balls. This also led me to a chance meeting with Adam Adams, who in turn, offered me something to do.

I could have done a lot of things that day as I saw the '57 T-Bird speeding towards me. I could have hidden in the weeds and he would never have seen me. I could have run away, and he would have never spoken to me. I could have given him the golf balls I had found, and never returned to the vacant lot or driving range. However, I chose to stay and face him.

So I said yes to Adam Adams; I would find the lost golf balls and hit them out for free. This began my first job. I went there every day after school, picked up balls, and hit them out for free for the next seven years (from ages nine to sixteen). Mr. Adams also started mentoring me and teaching me how to play golf. At twelve years old, I was breaking ninety for eighteen holes consistently, and at age fifteen, chosen to play on the high-school varsity golf team.

As the years progressed, my responsibilities increased to driving the tractor that picked up the golf balls, and working behind the desk selling buckets of golf balls to customers. Growing up in this environment gave me an insight into not just people, but adult people. The driving range was a busy place, and I really enjoyed being around the customers, who, for the most part, were successful middle and upper-middle-class folks. There were also some TV personalities and sports figures; it was really cool working there.

While at the driving range, I catered to the customers' needs, such as sodas, snacks, and bringing them more golf balls to hit out. I also kept them safe while they practiced their golf game. The driving range can be a dangerous place with all those golf clubs swinging and golf balls flying. We had people hit with golf clubs and golf balls on occasion;

they can really hurt you. But I did my best; I was constantly observant to anything that could potentially harm my customers. I believe it was here, growing up at the driving range, that my passion for keeping people safe was born.

Therefore, when I started college in 1970, I chose a career in law enforcement by majoring in criminology. A couple of years later, I began my career as a police officer. I learned from my years at the driving range that I liked people, and I liked keeping people safe from harm; this was my passion. So, at age twenty-one, I chose to dedicate my life to public service as a law enforcement officer. My feelings were that I could somehow make the world, or at least my city, a safer place to live.

As a police officer in my city, I kept myself in perfect physical shape by working out with weights five days a week and being an expert shot with a gun. I felt like I was more than equipped to handle any type of situation or altercation that might arise during my shift.

However, I was wrong. Knowing about the questionable tactics used by some rogue cops in the department, and not wanting to be a part of their group, led to my firing. The negative impact of "trial by media" was also used by these rogue cops to further damage my reputation. Stripped of my profession, then thrown back into society to fend for myself, was all that remained of my law enforcement career.

The choices I made in life moving forward would center around minimizing responsibility while maximizing enjoyment. The perfect vehicle for this was the Miami bar business: accountable only to the patrons sitting at my bar, while drinking my life away without a care in the world.

However, there were consequences with this type of lifestyle that would hurl me into the depths of my journey. But I think it was there that I found myself again.

REFLECTING

No matter what event in my life led to the decline of my integrity, I was always accountable for the decisions I made, good or bad. Since my release from federal prison twenty-eight years ago, I have worked extremely hard to become a productive member of society, and more importantly, to create a good example.

In short, I feel ashamed of my behavior leading up to my federal conviction, and will never act contra to the laws of our government again.

Analogously speaking, I basically slapped Uncle Sam (the father of our country) in the face by breaking the law. At that point, Uncle Sam swept my legs from beneath me by taking everything, including my freedom. As a result, I lay flat on my back with virtually nothing but a pulse. Then, Uncle Sam extended his hand and offered a chance to build a new life—the right way.

How do you begin to repay such compassion and forgiveness? The wonderful life Sheri and I are now living, I would have never known existed. During my educational journey, each corner I turned was met with a paved road. By "paved road," I mean an opportunity to proceed, a way to advance, a format set in place by our government that gives even the disobedient a route back.

In the preceding pages, I've shared with you the opportunities I have been afforded and the progress I have made in transforming a wasted life into something meaningful. It was the federal system that completely changed my life from bartender to eminent PhD.

I'm only a success because our country has a mechanism in place that can transform wayward individuals into valuable citizens.

MY DAD AND WORLD WAR II

Our veterans fought for, and brought to fruition, the ideals our country stands for. Our flag and its stars and stripes represent America, and all who live in its shadow are protected by Americans.

My Dad was a left waist gunner in a B-17 Flying Fortress and fought during World War II. He climbed into the belly of the "Maiden USA" (the name of his aircraft) thirty-three times before being shot down over Anzio Beach, Italy. He spent the next fourteen months near starvation in a German prisoner-of-war camp in different locations in Germany and Italy. He woke up one morning to find a jeep with a big star on the side sitting at the front gate of his prison camp. He and his comrades had finally been liberated. He weighed ninety pounds.

My dad returned home to Tampa, Florida, and was reunited with his mom, dad, and brothers. He had been gone for about two years. During that period of time, his mom's hair had gone from solid black to solid white; he was very much missed. Four years later, my dad would find himself with a new wife and a new baby girl. One year later, he added a baby boy to his new family. My dad kept his old flying suit in the closet right up front; his army footlocker lay directly beneath his flying suit locked up on the floor, but he never spoke about either one—ever. Dad would stay up nights in his recliner watching old WWII documentaries all through the 1950s, '60s, '70s, and '80s, but he never spoke about his years in Europe.

I spoke to him about the war and his contributions and sacrifices a few years before his death. It was after I had endured the tumultuous years of my youth. I wanted to put into perspective the sacrifices he and his fellow veterans had made during the war, and how we all grew to reap the benefits of growing up and living in America. I was speaking directly about me and how I was given a second chance to make something of myself, and the gift of being able to do that was something that was bought and paid for with the blood, sweat, and tears of our veterans. I wanted him to hear and see me say thank you.

Picture Twenty-One: Dad in WWII Army Air Corp Uniform

We live in a country that encourages us to dream and create; therefore, in this life, anything's possible.

I wanted the Army Rangers to feel special, and the only way I could do this was to make their environment look special by cutting grass.

Now I want them to be safe, along with all our loved ones in the military. I can do this now, too, by designing world-class electronic circuits that operate our country's defense systems.

The twenty-hour bus ride back to Miami gave me time to relive my life. I stepped off that bus feeling empowered, and understood exactly what I needed to do. I would take all the hope and direction given to me by Harold Owens and the guys at the shop, and couple it with the confidence and determination of my youth.

It's just like when I shot the gun out of the guy's hand when I was a policeman. I had it in my mind that I was not going to hurt that guy. I was confident that I could place a bullet anywhere I wanted; I chose to hit the firing pin of his weapon. I killed the gun and saved the guy for his family by being confident, focused, and determined to control the outcome of that situation.

Now it's time to once again control the outcome of this situation, this situation being my life, and how I move forward from here.

APPENDIX

Police Guns Drop Robbers At S&L

Herald Staff Writer

The policemen made no move to interrupt the robbery as it was taking place Friday. Having already waited a week for this holdup, they figured they could wait a few more minutes.

As a result, the shootout that followed jeopardized no customers or employes of the Savings & Loan Association branch office. That happened outside, as the bandits fled with a bag of cash.

All three ignored the surrender order, police said. All three were felled by police bullets. One died instantly.

Two other suspects, _____ were wounded in the exchange of gunfire with police. _____ was reported in good condition at _____ Hospital; _____ was listed as critical at _____ Hospital.

_____ police received an anonymous telephone tip last week that the branch, _____ was going to be robbed.

13 plainclothes officers from both departments began watching the bank last Friday.

Armed with shotguns and portable radios, officers were spread out around the bank. Two shared a front porch observation post with an elderly man who lives near the bank.

The police strategy focused on apprehending the suspects after they left the bank, to minimize the chance of injury. Though a plainclothes detective was in the bank during the r o b b e r y, police said, the strategy still remained the same because other officers had surrounded the outside of the bank.

POLICE SAID the three men, wearing surgical gloves and ski masks, entered the bank at about 10 a.m. after parking a late model Pontiac in a driveway near the front door. The engine was left running as the men entered the bank.

"The police yelled to them to 'Freeze — Stop, Police.'" "They didn't stop. One of them pointed his gun at a policeman and then the others did and the shooting began."

Police had briefed the bank's 15 employes that a robbery might be attempted. The employes were instructed to cooperate with the robbers and not attempt to interfere.

Wednesday, police said, at least two of the suspects visited the bank to "case the place." They were observed then and officers recognized them when they returned Friday.

Police said the suspects entered the bank, "waving their guns," and ordered employes and customers to "kneel down."

ONE OF THE bandits, police said, carried a bag from one teller cage to another, gathering money.

"The police did a good job — no one got hurt — and I was happy to help them." _____ who conceded he was "a little nervous" while watching the gun battle.

Article One: Police Guns Drop Robbers At S&L

Police Didn't Recognize Him

Man Slain During Holdup Identified as an Informer

Herald Staff Writer

⊒ The man police killed during a savings and loan robbery Friday turned out to be a confidential informant who had tipped them about the robbery.

"It's not good from my standpoint. We couldn't have been more careful

Chief
said.
"I hated to see it happen. It's embarrassing."

died in a hail of buckshot from police weapons as he and two others ran from the midmorning robbery of the   Federal Savings and Loan Association's branch office

"ORIGINALLY the informant was told he was not going to participate. He advised us that he was not going to participate. He advised

Turn to Page 17A Col. 1

Holdup Suspect Dies Behind Police Line Outside   Federal's   Branch

Article Two: Man Slain During Holdup Identified as an Informer

Police Killed Informer
In   Bank Robbery

> **FROM PAGE 1**

us that he was not going to be involved,"

_____ said he personally told _____ not to participate in the robbery after detective _____ introduced

Because the three men who robbed the store wore ski masks, _____ police didn't realize until after the gunfire that the dead man was their informant.

Two other men — _____ .·.

_____ — were wounded in the shoot-out with 13 _____ policemen who had staked out the bank.

_____ was in serious condition Monday in the jail ward in _____ Hospital. _____ was released from the ward to the Dade County Jail. Both are charged in the robbery.

_____ began cooperating with police and state prosecutors after he was arrested for another robbery,

IN THAT earlier robbery, _____

were charged with holding up the

It was after this that _____ said he introduced _____ to the chief.

_____ police had staked out the savings and loan last Tuesday when a car suspected as a potential robbery vehicle drove up.

But the robbery was foiled when a security guard routinely asked the men to park the car properly,

Last Thursday evening, _____ telephoned again, saying the robbery was going to be at the savings and loan the next day.

"HE SAID, 'It's gonna go,' b u t he didn't know the car or the time because _____ didn't say which car would be used. _____ didn't trust anyone,"

At 10:11 a.m. last Friday, a late-model Pontiac drove up to the side window of the savings and loan. _____ police were on rooftops and in private houses prepared to block traffic if necessary. _____ they also were prepared to stop the robbers before they entered the bank and charge them with "conspiracy to commit a robbery."

The stakeout officers didn't realize the robbers had arrived until they saw them leave the Pontiac in a "skip, hop and a jump,"

The three men wore ski masks and surgical gloves.

INSIDE THE bank, _____ detective _____ posed as a bank executive. He had a voice-activated tape player with him.

_____ replayed the tape Monday. He identified the voices of the robbers.

"Good morning," one of the voices said. Then: "All right, give us the money. No, no. Don't touch that. All the paper money. That's it. Get it in there."

The tape lasted scarcely two minutes. Then the shooting started.

Police and a witness said the three men, by then fleeing, turned their guns toward the officers after they were told to halt.

One man _____ started back toward the bank, according to _____ All three were shot. _____ died at the scene.

"I CAN'T cover him once he went in the bank,"

"He even told me that if he was forced to go in, he wouldn't. He knew our layout. He could have stayed in the bank."

"Why he didn't drop his gun, I don't know,"

"We thought he was going back for hostages. We didn't want any hostages,"

_____ an assistant medical examiner, said _____ died of multiple shotgun wounds. Only the police were armed with shotguns.

Prosecutor _____ said an inquest will be held.

Article Three: Police Killed Informer In My City's Bank Robbery

Inspection Set of Files On Officer

Herald Staff Writer

Two lawyers who accused a policeman of misusing informants and falsifying reports Monday asked a judge to privately inspect the state's investigative files on the case.

Circuit Judge agreed to look at the files of the State Attorney's investigation of detective who resigned last Tuesday.

Judge said she would view the files Friday morning. The prosecutor objectded to the move, saying the files are confidential.

a became the focus of an investigation after . an assistant public defender, and uncovered what they claimed was evidence that misused his police powers.

who police say they shot after a robbery last March at the Savings and Loan office

A third man shot in the alleged robbery, said to be an informant for was shot also and died.

face trial for the robbery and a charge of illegal possession of weapons.

b said he intends to show that his client, was the victim of police entrapment in the robbery.

said in court that he gave the State Attorney's office information that may have set up informants only to arrest them to boost his own "fame and reputation."

asked Judge to examine the state files to determine if there is additional evidence similar to that he hopes to introduce at trial.

BECAUSE THE state has access to some reports which are not available to him, said he was unable to fully follow through with his investigation.

Both Administrative Assistant State Attorney Janet Reno and prosecutor opposed the move to inspect the files.

"The investigation is still pending, and the information is confidential," Miss Reno said. "We have made no judgment one way or the other," she said.

She declined to say when the investigation would be completed.

c told evidence that made false reports in three narcotics cases and misused informants in other cases.

lawyer declined comment. He said his client was under subpena and that the case was still pending in court.

Article Four: Inspection Set of Files On Officer

101

Lawyer: Victim Had No Mask

a An assistant Dade public defender said Wednesday he has a photograph that shows slain informant wore no mask in the March 21 robbery of a savings and loan office as police claim.

b The lawyer, has been working on the case since was killed by the police who hired him as an informant and provided the car he used in the robbery.

reiterated Wednesday that his officers saw the three men wear masks when they entered the savings and loan.

c THE policemen involved testified at an inquest that the three men wore ski masks. The judge ruled the shooting was justified.

d But said a photo he obtained from FBI files shows inside the savings and loan without a mask.

And said he has a statement from a witness who did not testify at the inquest that he saw without a mask outside the savings and loan.

Although wore the clothes police instructed him to wear and used the police-provided car, said his men did not recognize

e said his witness was near the front of the savings and loan when police opened fire as the robbers left.

THE TWO other men accused in the robbery — — will be tried later. is gathering information for use in that trial, he said, and he will present the photo as evidence. would not divulge the name of the witness.

Article Five: Lawyer: Victim Had No Mask

Detective Is Investigation Target

Herald Staff Writer

a The Dade state attorney's office and the _____ Police Department are investigating charges that an award-winning detective known for his aggressive police work misused informants and claimed to have witnessed crimes he never saw.

The target of the inquiries is _____ a former Metro patrolman who joined the force in 1973 where he served as chief detective.

b _____ resigned his post effective Tuesday after _____ relieved the detective of his official duties last week.

c According to _____ executive assistant to Dade State Attorney Richard Gerstein, the investigation began after several lawyers in that office complained about _____ handling of cases, including allegations that _____ charged several persons with drug sales the detective knew they never made, used improper procedures to identify criminal suspects and misused police informants.

d "WHETHER SLOPPY police work is involved or deception remains to be seen." _____ Wednesday that his own departmental investigation had uncovered one confirmed instance of official misconduct by _____ to date.

e "We have determined," _____ "that in one instance _____ and _____ patrolman _____ took out a warrant on a burglar and did not execute the warrant but continued to use the suspect as an informant which to say the least is a no no."

Neither _____ nor his attorney could be reached for comment Wednesday.

_____ flatly denied _____ allegation. "To the best of my knowledge, I have never misued an informant."

A patrolman assigned to the detective division of the _____ force, _____ has voluntarily given a statement to the state attorney's office regarding his relationship with _____

f BOTH OFFICERS have worked together on a number of cases including the robbery at the _____ Federal Saving and Loan office last March which resulted in the death of police informant _____

At an inquest into _____ death, _____ and _____ admitted discussing the robbery with _____ prior to the commission of the crime. The informant and two other men drove to the bank in an unmarked car on loan from the _____ Police Department.

g _____ and _____ the men accused of robbing the bank with _____ is scheduled to begin Monday.

Lawyers for the defendants have let it be known that they intend to question the credibility and professional conduct of _____ during the trial.

_____ police chief _____ said Wednesday he was convinced "the robbery was handled in a very professional manner. We have nothing to be ashamed of." He called _____ a "high-class law enforcement officer; very capable and honest."

Article Six: Detective Is Investigation Target

103

Officer Takes 5th on 20 Questions

a Former   policeman under pressure in December, invoked the Fifth Amendment Friday to questions about a robbery in which police shot their own informant.

invoked the privilege 20 times to questions asked by

lawyers representing

are charged in the robbery last March at the   Savings and Loan Association in which police informant   was shot and killed.

b Friday's hearing was to clarify   position at a deposition last month in which he refused to answer questions by (and refused to invoke his Fifth Amendment privilege against self-incrimination. b

invoked the privilege Friday on advice of his lawyer. he said.

Circuit Judge | recessed the hearing until January 26 when she will rule on   request that   not be required to answer the questions.

c   resigned from the   department after the State Attorney's office announced it was investigating allegations that he misused informants and fabricated evidence.

d   may have encouraged   to set up the robbery as well.

questions apparently were aimed at determining if (has supplied informants with drugs and finding out the nature of Chisolm's resignation from the Metro police department in April, 1973.

After   said he would invoke the Fifth Amendment to all questions,   cut his questions short.

At the previous deposition,   asked more than 100 questions of   Friday, he asked fewer than 20 questions.

will be tried Feb. 2.

Article Seven: Officer Takes 5th on 20 Questions

EDITORIALS

Slaying of Police Informant Raises Questions on Tactics

THE POLICE informant's life is dangerous at best; one tiny slip and those he is informing on may kill him without warning. But when an informant is killed by incompetent police who set up the crime that took his life, something ought to be done to protect both the informants and the propriety of police operations.

Fortunately, something is being done about the fiasco in which police killed their own informant in Friday night's stakeout at the Restaurant. State Attorney Janet Reno has ordered an investigation and assigned her executive assistant, to conduct it.

We trust that a lawyer known for his aggressiveness, will find out why police, for the second time in less than three years, killed their own informant in a stakeout.

There is more to be asked here than what went wrong with the plans the police had worked out with the 19-year-old informant. The police have not been exactly forthcoming with answers. We hope will spur them to be.

But the inexcusable killing of tragic though it was, is also symptomatic of a police philosophy that needs to be set aright.

We do not question the necessity for law-enforcement agencies to recruit, maintain, and protect a network of informants. Without informants, many police investigations would get nowhere.

Nor do we question the necessity for informants, to protect their anonymity, sometimes to participate in crimes about which they are informing police. That necessity is as self-evident as the need for informants themselves.

But should the police plot with their informant a crime that might otherwise not have occurred? We think not. Yet the available evidence indicates that detectives encouraged in luring two other men into attempting to rob the Restaurant.

The dead informant's mother says her son talked on the phone with detectives several times on Friday, perfecting arrangements for the stakeout and robbery. viewed himself as being cast in a *Mission: Impossible* role. Little did he know.

It is one thing for police, told by an informant that a crime is to be committed, to stake out the scene and attempt to prevent it. But it comes perilously close to entrapment for police to instigate the crime through their informant. Entrapment or not, the practice is clearly improper and should be stopped.

Article Eight: Slaying of Police Informant Raises Questions on Tactics

Police Killed Own Informant

Marcus Stern Writer

Fascinated by the "Mission Impossible" intrigue of undercover work, a teenage police buff modeled a robbery mask for his mother, told her not to worry — and several hours later died in a hail of police bullets and shotgun blasts.

a ___ 19, is the second police informant killed in less than three years by the detectives with whom he had worked.

b ___ who was fascinated by electronics equipment and police work, had planned the robbery for days with detectives.

C HE HAD PROUDLY showed his mother adhesive tape marks on his stomach where police had taped a concealed microphone, she said Saturday. He modeled a mask made from his sister's swim cap that he said detectives told him to wear.

"He was fascinated," his mother said. "He was playing 'Mission Impossible.' He loved electronics."

d "Don't worry, Mommy," she quoted him as saying Friday night.

"I'm going to be in the driver's seat and they (the police) know it. The others will be inside. I'll be outside. The detectives showed me how to do everything."

e ___ worked with the informant in the 1975 ___ stakeout. ___ also was involved in an operation in which a ___ police informant was slain by police.

___ ment Saturday.

___ was the first to open fire Friday night — killing the 17-year-old who allegedly pointed a rifle at him, police said.

___ the informant, failed to follow their instructions "to leave the area immediately." They refused to answer other questions.

Police Chief ___ told a reporter to "read the reports we've already made on it, if you want to know about that." He then hung up. His subordinates refused to

Article Nine: Police Killed Own Informant

Cops Kill Own Informant

▶ FROM PAGE 1A

provide the reports.

mother said he'd confided the robbery plan to her. She said he had been told to remain in the car until his companions were arrested. Then he would be ordered to step out, walk forward slowly and have his hands handcuffed behind his back.

That would maintain his cover as an informant and prevent reprisals, his mother said. Afterward he would be freed, she said.

In return, police promised him probation on a pending burglary charge, $200 for the undercover work and a job in the police department communications section, the parents said.

had been charged in January with burglary in a case involving stolen electronics parts, police said.

"HE WOULDN'T take the $200," said his mother. "He told them he would give it back to the fund for the children of police officers killed on duty."

He left Friday after numerous telephone conversations with the detectives, she said.

said the detectives were pressing for the robbery to be done Friday night. "They didn't want to wait," she said.

Her son gave her two numbers to call — one for Robbery Detective who had referred him to and the other — if he did not arrive home by 1:15 a.m.

When she called, she said, the detectives would not talk to her.

Her son was already dead at Doctors Hospital of multiple gunshot wounds.

"They all knew he was the informant." Police spokesman said. "They were probably just trying to stop the car."

THE DRIVER'S side of brown 1974 Grand Prix was riddled with bullets. Emergency room workers could not see how many times was shot, they said, because he was drenched in blood.

tol. At least four shotgun blasts were fired. The driver's side was ripped by slugs, and was wounded, police said.

"It didn't turn out the way we thought it would," one detective admitted at the scene.

In March 1975, and police shot three men as they emerged from a savings and loan robbery.

slain by police shotguns, was the informant in that robbery for police. He was driving a car provided by police.

Officer Checks Car in Which Teen Was Shot
...he died later at Doctors Hospital
— SKIP HERE / Miami Herald Staff

Article Nine (Continued): Police Killed Own Informant

Reno Will Probe Fatal Stakeout

Herald Staff Writer

a Dade State Attorney Janet Reno ordered an investigation Sunday of the stakeout in which detectives killed two teenagers, one of them their own informant, whose skull they shattered with shotgun blasts.

"I want to know exactly what happened," Reno said. She assigned her executive assistant ... to conduct the probe.

b ... was hit near- ly 10 times by police slugs as he sat behind the wheel of his car in front of the ... Restaurant. ... He and ... detectives had plan- ned a robbery-arrest at the popular restaurant.

... for days, the boy's parents and police said. c

HE WAS TO drive his own car and remain outside. His two companions would be arrested inside.

... was shot in the face, just above the left eyebrow, moments after walking into the restaurant's foyer, at 11:40 p.m. Friday.

Detective ... shot him with a .357 magnum. Metro police said. ... and told Metro investigators that ... failed to obey orders to freeze and then lifted a sawed-off .22-caliber rifle.

Other detectives outside opened fire on the driver's side of ... car, killing him. Only ... survived.

... and other detectives had met ... after Metro Robbery Detective ... referred him to ... police.

with

d POLICE CALLED ... at home numerous times Friday. His mother said they told him to bring a mask.

Police said they opened fire on the car when ... dashed out and dove in the passenger's side window.

e He was promised $200, a job in the police communications bureau and short probation on a burglary charge, the parents said.

... also was a principal in a 1975 stakeout in which ... police killed their own informant.

f ... The informant, who tipped them to the robbery, was driving a car provided by police. Two other robbers who survived wounds from that robbery said the informant had set up and initiated the robbery.

Article Ten: Reno Will Probe Fatal Stakeout

Reno Passes Informant Shooting To Grand Jury, Coroner Inquest

Herald Staff Writer

Dade State Attorney Janet Reno passed the investigation of the fatal shooting of a teenage police informant to the Grand Jury and to a coroner's inquest Monday.

"Crediting her staff with "one of the most thorough investigations this office has ever conducted," Reno said at a Metro Justice Building press conference that "we want to leave no stone unturned ... in making the public aware of what happened."

The inquest, scheduled for 10 a.m. Friday before Magistrate Ed

Newbold, will reveal results of a two-week probe of the shooting of _____ by a policeman during a robbery stakeout Feb. 17.

RENO REFUSED to discuss, at the press conference, the filing of possible criminal charges against police at the stakeout or against the only alleged robber to survive the shooting.

But, by petitioning for a coroner's inquest before taking the case to the Grand Jury, Reno has protected several options:

• If Newbold finds probable

cause that _____ police negligently killed _____ Reno could file criminal charges, probably manslaughter.

• If Newbold decides that the shooting was justified, the state attorney could ignore the finding and file charges. Or, Reno could accept the magistrate's decision and close the investigation. while avoiding public suggestions of a whitewash.

• Regardless of the coroner's finding, Reno could seek a Grand Jury indictment. The Grand Jury also could return a no true bill.

"Obviously, the judge's finding is going to have a bearing on what I do," said Reno.

Unless the grand jury returns an indictment. Reno will decide whether charges will be filed. The inquest judges' decision is advisory, but the inquest allows prosecutors to publicly present information, such as hearsay and evidence of other crimes, that often is barred from use in criminal trials.

"NO DETERMINATION has been made at this point as to whether or when they (criminal charges) will be filed," said Reno.

Veteran prosecutors on the state attorney's staff apparently are divided about the case. Last week, 18 prosecutors who reviewed details of the shooting voted 10-to-8 in a straw poll to recommend no police prosecution.

Reno said she personally viewed the shooting scene. Chief Assistant _____ questioned five of the six policemen at the stakeout, reviewed hundreds of photographs and diagrams of the area and interviewed eyewitnesses.

Officer _____ who fired the shotgun blast that apparently killed Garcia. refused last week to testify without immunity from prosecution.

_____ was hit by at least nine shotgun pellets as he drove a getaway car from the _____ Restaurant, the scene of the aborted robbery.

Another alleged robber, _____ in the restaurant from a police gun shot after he allegedly raised a .22-caliber rifle when confronted by police.

Reno called the shooting of _____ "a tragedy."

The state attorney said the Grand Jury will also be asked to probe the "practices, policies and procedures" used by _____ police when planning the stakeout with _____

RENO SAID SHE will meet with _____ Police Chief _____ about "recommendations to prevent similar shootings.

Reno is expected to ask that _____ police contact the state attorney's office when planning stakeouts.

The Grand Jury also will investigate another shooting involving _____ police.

_____ was fired upon by _____ police Feb. 2 when he unknowingly drove through a roadblock. Reno called the shooting "a near tragedy."

Reno said she is still seeking results of crime lab tests which will show how far _____ was from the car and how _____ was holding the shotgun.

Article Eleven: Reno Passes Informant Shooting To Grand Jury, Coroner Inquest